THE HEART GOD
HEARS

WES DAUGHENBAUGH

Gospel Net Ministries
P.O. box 34777
Omaha, NE 68134

©1980 Gospel Net Ministries
Updated ©1996 Gospel Net Ministries

Third printing, revised and expanded, Nov. 1996
Retitled—The Heart God HEARS
©1996 by Gospel Net Ministries
ISBN# 0-9655471-0-8
Illustrations by Dave Wilson, Gary Grubbs
Desktop Publishing, Freestyle Graphics, Omaha, NE.
Cover Design by Adfiliation, Eugene, Oregon.

CONTENTS

FORWARD

Suppose a person asks God, "Lord, how could I maximize my effectiveness upon this earth for your plan, purpose, and persuasion?" I believe God would answer in this manner. "Be careful for nothing but in everything by prayer and supplication with thanksgiving let your request be made known unto God," (Philippians 4:6 KJV).

In the late 1960's everyone was singing the popular song "What the world needs now, is love, sweet love. It's the only thing that there's just too little of." I would change those lyrics to say, "What the world needs now is prayer, more prayer. It's the only thing there is just too little of."

Philippians 4:6 deals with intercession. Intercession can move mountains, lift them up and cast them into the sea. Intercession can stop rain for three and a half years, and that same intercession can restart that rain. (James 5:17-18, speaking of Elijah's prayers.) Intercession can save a nation according to 2 Chronicles 2:14. I've seen intercession heal marriages, start churches, launch ministries, save the lost, and loose people from the grip of death.

During the years when God taught Wes many of the lessons in this book, I was privileged to be on his bus ministry staff. (You'll find reference to me on page 46.) I was the ex-alcoholic who helped him figure out a prayer of intercession for a wayward pastor.

I was also a recipient of these "foundational truths." Wes refused to see me as the world saw me—or as many Christians viewed me. Seeing me through God's eyes, Wes treated me as valuable, precious, and useful for ministry. After reading these pages you'll understand "the equipping of the saints" (Ephesians 4:11-12) in a much clearer way.

One of the most powerful books ever written on the subject of prayer and intercession, *The Heart God Hears,* goes to the very core of the problems that hinder prayer. I have personally given many copies of this book (formerly *Foundations of Intercession*) to friends in the ministry for more effective and dynamic results in their calling.

I wholeheartedly and unreservedly recommend this book to every apostle, prophet, evangelist, pastor, and teacher for a more productive ministry and to every member of the Body of Christ for more effective sojourning on this earth.

This book is packed with God's truths. Read them and do them, and I guarantee positive change in your walk and ministry.

Rev. Patrick L. Burgess, Ph.D.

International Overseer of Loving Faith Fellowship
    International

Pastor of Loving Faith Fellowship, Sioux City, Iowa

---

*This book is Dedicated
to all who love Jesus Christ
and the Word of God.*

"May they be brought to complete
unity to let the world know that you
sent me [Jesus] and have loved them
even as you have loved me."
(John 17:23, NIV)

INTRODUCTION

I was stricken with panic. The most spiritual young man in my Bible college dorm had just asked me to pray for my roommate to be healed. As the guys gathered around, thoughts rushed through my head, "He won't be healed when you pray. Then everyone will know how faithless you are." My roommate's problem wasn't too serious—only a headache that had bothered him all day long. Still, I had hoped no one would ask me to pray for Del.

Suddenly I remembered the scripture, "This is the confidence we have in approaching God: that if we ask anything according to his will, he hears us. And if we know that he hears us—whatever we ask—we know that we have what we asked of him," (1 John 5;14-15 NIV). That was what I needed. If I could just get God to hear my prayer—then my roommate would be healed.

Desperately I began my prayer, "Oh God, hear us!" I paused, unsure if God was listening. To be real sure, I prayed again, "Oh God, hear us!" I paused again. I just had to be sure he was listening because if he heard me, the healing would happen. To be absolutely certain of an answer, I prayed the third time, "Oh God, hear us!"

At that moment Del threw up his hands and began to rejoice, "I'm healed! I'm healed! I felt Jesus touch me on the head. The pain is all gone." He insisted Jesus or an angel had physically touched him. None of us had. Wow! I never even got to pray my prayer. What an unforgettable experience.

If God hears you— you've got your prayer answered!

When Christ stood before the tomb of Lazarus, he said, "Father, I thank you that you have heard me. I knew that you always hear me," (John 11:41-42 NIV). He hadn't even prayed his prayer yet or commanded Lazarus to rise. But it was a done deal. God always heard Jesus—and if God hears, the prayer is answered.

Does God hear everybody when they pray?

No. "When I called, they did not listen; so when they called, I would not listen; says the Lord Almighty," (Zachariah 7:13 NIV). God always listened to Jesus because Jesus always listened to God and obeyed him.

What about us? Can we pray with the kind of confidence that Christ prayed when he stood before Lazarus' tomb? Yes, we can, but there is a condition—the condition of our hearts!

"Dear friends, if our hearts do not condemn us, we have confidence before God and receive from him anything we ask, because we obey his commands and do what pleases him," (1 John 3:21 NIV).

When we pray and our hearts are condemning us because we haven't forgiven someone, or we know we've been judging people, or we've been refusing to reconcile, or we want to stay angry at our mate and treat them with disrespect and inconsideration—God just doesn't hear as good! Prayers are hindered.

"Husbands...be considerate as you live with your wives, and treat them with respect...so that nothing will hinder your prayers," (1 Peter 3:7 NIV).

Too often Christians are looking for printed prayers that will say just the right words—magic words God will hear. The trouble is, God hears not only the basis of what is said, but on the condition of the heart offering the prayer.

Do you want to be the kind of person God always hears? Then you must allow God to work on your heart until it is one that doesn't condemn you when you pray. That's what this book is all about.

An intercessor—one who can get answered prayers not just for himself but for others.

Over the years God has taught me many lessons that have prepared me to live the life of an intercessor—one who can get answered prayers not just for myself, but for others. A great many of the "lessons" came in the form of God's loving rebukes.

As a confused young man on my way to Bible college, God spoke to me through Proverbs 1:23, "Turn at my rebuke. Surely, I will pour out my Spirit on you; I will make my words known to you," (NKJV). That is what I needed—and what you need. You'll overcome your problems if God's Spirit is poured out on you and his words are made known to you. Faith, wisdom, guidance, etc. come when we hear God's words.

This sounded so good to me I made a covenant with God and vowed to turn at his rebuke. While traveling through the Columbia River Gorge, I prayed, "God, I make a covenant with you on this river. If you will take the time to rebuke me, I vow that I will turn at your rebuke. As often as you look down from heaven and see this great river gorge, remember that Wes will turn at you rebuke."

God took me at my word. One kind, gentle, life-giving rebuke after another began to come to me. God's words are so loving and so wise they do not minister any condemnation. I love them. This book contains a treasury of loving corrections God has given to my heart.

Get ready to hear God speak to you in these chapters. Listen to him sincerely and diligently apply these truths. Then when you speak, God will hear you. You'll pray with new confidence, not just because you said the right things, but because you will have become the kind of person God delights in hearing.

This book was formerly called *Foundations of Intercession* because each chapter lays a foundation stone of truth upon which to build a life of effective prayer. Each chapter deals with a hindrance to prayer and gives you truth to overcome that hindrance.

You may be thinking, "I just want to get my prayer answered. I don't care about being an intercessor." That's wrong thinking. Here's why.

Christ gave the best definition for success when he prayed, "I have brought you glory on earth by completing the work you gave me to do," (John 17:4 NIV). Meaning in life, purpose in life, and satisfaction in life all revolve around bringing glory to God.

If you love God—you will crave to bring him glory. Massive glory.

We can bring God five kinds of glory: 1) Basic glory 2) Added glory 3) Multiplied glory 4) Great glory and 5) Compounded interest glory.

Basic glory is brought to God when you live in kindness and consideration for others. *Added glory* comes when you win a soul to Christ and someone is added to the kingdom. *Multiplied glory* comes to God when we train leaders. In the early church even when 5,000 were saved at a time they were only *added* to the church. But in Acts chapter six leaders (deacons) were raised up. Then the number of disciples was *multiplied.*

Great glory comes when we pray and through our prayers open a door for God to become involved in human affairs and do the really great big things—like bring a national revival! *Compound interest glory* is brought to God by constantly being faithful over a lifetime. Put them all together, and you get massive glory to God!

One night in a prayer meeting I got a "fax from God," as I call it. God beamed into my spirit the knowledge that this craving I feel to bring God massive glory is actually a call to prayer. Without effective prayer, massive glory can never be brought to God. No wonder God wants each of his children to become Christlike intercessors who capture God's attention every time we pray! We don't learn these truths just to benefit ourselves. We learn them to honor and glorify our wonderful Heavenly Father.

We live in perilous times. The world economy may soon crash under the weight of accumulated debt. Rogue nations possess nuclear warheads and with the increase of technology will soon have the capability to threaten any city on earth via their rockets. Evil forces are stirring again in Russia. America lies in a complacent slumber unaware of swiftly approaching catastrophic judgement for its sins. I'm convinced we must have revival for survival.

We must have revival for survival.

To have revival we must have a great prayer movement. To have an effective prayer movement we must have intercessors to whom God will listen. Would you devote yourself to becoming the heart God always hears and join the army of end-time intercessors God is raising up? May it be so.

1
THE IMPORTANCE OF SOUL-WINNING

Every layman is called of God to minister in three areas: l) soul-winning, 2) intercession, and 3) cheerful giving.

In this book we'll be dealing with the ministry of what I call "Basic Intercession." First, we must look briefly at the ministry of the soul-winner. All Christians must move into the ministry of a soul-winner. Why? Because if they don't, they will never excel in the areas of intercession and cheerful giving.

From the day I fell deeply in love with Christ and the Word of God, I wanted to be used of God in a great way to bring glory to his name. After graduating from Bible college, I went to work in a veneer mill in western Oregon. Each day, while doing the monotonous job of pulling veneer off the green chain, I'd dream about being used of God. When I got home after the exhausting ten-hour day, only about four hours were left before bedtime. After having supper and talking to my young bride for a while, I was so tired I had to go to sleep. This went on for days while the desire to be used of God grew more intense.

Finally, one night I sank down on my knees in our small living room and prayed, "Oh God, if you'd just use me! If all you let me do is to shine some pastor's shoes, I'd be so grateful!" I meant it with all my heart. No job would have been insignificant. I wanted to be used of God so badly.

God took me at my word. A few days later the pastor of a local church phoned me and asked us to come talk to him. Although he didn't know me, this pastor offered me the job of directing the adult choir. He also wanted my wife to become the church pianist. Although I had never directed a choir before and didn't read music, I told him I'd give it a try.

On Saturday mornings, I led our choir practice and on Sundays led songs and directed choir. It felt so good to be doing something for God. This went on for several weeks, and then that familiar longing in my spirit to do something great for God began to return—this time stronger than before.

Finally, in desperation, I cried out to God and said, "Just what is my ministry supposed to be, anyway?"

God spoke to my spirit, "Your ministry here is to be a soul-winner."

The Good Ground

I began seeking God as to how to become a soul-winner. It is possible to have many "ministries" in the church and yet miss the main one. God began to teach me that to win a lot of souls, I should begin with children. He told me they were "the good ground" of Matthew 13, but that there was a time element involved. If the good ground sat around too long without being sown, weeds would come up and the ground would become hard.

God then led me by a series of events to become a bus captain and later a bus director. Thousands of children were signed up and brought under the influence of the Gospel. Later, I received training in personal soul-winning to adults. Home visitation teams then began to win parents of these children.

Our church experienced rapid growth and drew national attention. Our senior pastor became well known and began to travel around the nation and even to foreign fields.

After I became so involved in bus ministry, the church put me on full-time salary. It was not until I had spent several years in full-time ministry that I went to my knees to ask God if there was anything else. When our pastor began to be used of God in ever-widening circles, I asked God if he was calling me to be an evangelist or a prophet. His answer to me was, "Yes, there is something else I want you to become. I want you to become an intercessor."

Basic Training

Soul-winning is a training ground for the ministry of intercession. Had I not been faithful in soul-winning, I would never have had enough love to function as an intercessor. Nor would I have been disciplined enough.

God had already taught me many lessons that were necessary to "being" an intercessor. For many years I have practiced these until I live in this message and react by reflex as an intercessor. Still, what I will be sharing with you in this book are only the basics. God told me:

> "When you learn the lesson of basic intercession,
> deeper lessons will come to your heart.
> But till you intercede for your brother's small need,
> real travail you're not ready to start."

The deeper lessons of travail are starting to come to me.

Many Christians have touched the area of travail in prayer. They are robbed of prayer power, however. Why? *Because they allow disobedience, bitterness, and critical attitudes to be in their lives.* They are missing the basics.

Why is being a soul-winner necessary move into "basic intercession?" It is easier to love a lost person who has an excuse for being mean, irritable, domineering, selfish, etc., than it is to love a saved person who manifests these same character faults. There is no excuse for a Christian to act this way. It takes more love to love an imperfect Christian than it does to love an imperfect sinner. If we can't have compassion on the sinner, how in the world can we ever expect to have enough love to perfect the Christian who is not Christlike in character?

I have come to view "basic intercession" not as something you do occasionally, but as something you live and breathe twenty-four hours a day. It is something you are. You don't just do intercession, you are an intercessor.

God has shown me that if Christians can't even pray for the small need in a brother's life, they will lack the love and discipline it takes to wrestle in travail for lost souls. And, if they can't at least show enough concern to invite a lost person to church, or give a neighbor kid a ride to Sunday School, how will they have enough love to pray for their Christian brother who has faults? They won't.

This is exactly why so many churches split, vote out their pastors, fight over which color of toilet paper to put in the church bathrooms, etc. Divisive Christians are rarely soul-winners, people deeply concerned for the lost. Divisive Christians are definitely not intercessors. Intercessors are the sweet spirits in the church that bind the whole body together with love.

Who Is Qualified

If you don't have enough love to invite people to church and to share Christ with them, how will you ever have enough love to desire to give thousands of dollars to God's work? You'll love money more than souls and fail to move into the ministry of being a cheerful giver if you don't have a burden for lost souls and desire to win them! How tremendously important it is to be a soul-winner!

Some people excuse themselves from learning how to win souls by saying, "Oh, that's not my ministry. My ministry is prayer."

God told me differently. He told me that only the soul-winners qualify for a ministry of prayer. Those who don't care enough to do something about inviting people to church, teaching a class, doing a bus route, etc., will never care enough to move into intercession. Why? Because intercession is tougher! *You'll have no ministry in prayer if you aren't a soul-winner!*

POWER IS GENERATED THROUGH PRAISE, EDUCATION, FAITH, PRAYER, SPIRITUAL GIFTS, THE HOLY SPIRIT ETC. TO HELP US REACH THE GOAL—WINNING SOULS.

The rewards of a life of intercession are great. That's why I hope you will do something to identify yourself as one who is deeply concerned about souls. Then you can learn intercession at the same time you are learning to win souls.

Anyone can pass out tracts or leave good literature in laundromats. Anyone can give a neighbor kid a ride to church. (More people don't do this because the kid would probably want a ride the week they wanted to go to the beach or the mountains and skip church!) Many Christians could drive a bus, be a bus captain, or teach a Sunday School class. Everyone can tell others how wonderful it is to be saved. Giving your personal testimony is a powerful tool for winning others. But do something! Do something that marks you as a person deeply concerned over lost souls. It's not difficult.

Quality or Quantity?

All churches and individual Christians need to get their ministries in perspective. Soul-winning must be the goal! Prayer, faith, and the gifts of the Spirit help us to reach the goal. They must never become a goal in themselves. Power is generated in prayer to reach the goal of winning and keeping souls. Power is generated in the gifts of the Spirit to overcome all the obstacles that stand in the way of winning thousands to Christ.

Some churches, however, in an effort to attract the Charismatics, have made praise or healing or the Baptism of the Holy Spirit the emphasis of their church rather than soul-winning. Others have made education their goal. Praise, healing, the Holy Spirit, and education are all wonderful, but if they are put above soul-winning, your church will start moving toward false doctrine and/or spiritual sterility.

Those church people who say, "We want quality, not quantity," don't realize how ignorant that sounds.

When Jesus gave the great commission, he said, "Therefore, go and make disciples of all nations, baptizing them in the name of the Father, and of the Son, and of the Holy Spirit, and teaching them to obey everything I have commanded you," (Matthew 28:19-20, NIV).

When he said, "Make disciples of all nations," that was the command for quantity. Then, he made the command for quality, "...teaching them to obey everything I have commanded you."

We can't have just half of the great commission. If education becomes the goal, few souls will be won. But the church that wins souls naturally wants to educate them to keep them from falling away.

If we make praising God our goal rather than obeying God, will God enjoy the praise? The starting of a bus motor on Sunday morning sounds like praise to God's ears. When the alarm goes off at 5:00 a.m. and the bus director gets up, ready for a big day—that sounds like praise to God! When churches are building at God's command and the sound of hammers ascends to heaven, that sounds like praise to God. If you are a soul-winner who is helping God to achieve his goal of reaching the lost, then every little sound you make will sound like praise to God!

For five years my wife and I wanted a baby. When Bonnie delivered our first child, a seven pound, six ounce baby girl, we loved her so much that every little sound she made sounded precious to us. That is the way God loves soul-winners. He loves them so much, that the sound of their breathing sounds like praise! I'm certainly not against singing and praising. But, if you aren't working to win the lost, your praise has a hollow ring. It's empty of true love and devotion to the Lord!

The Goal

Why was the Holy Spirit poured out in the upper room? Because Jesus wanted his followers empowered so they could be great soul-winners! He was giving them supernatural power to reach the goal.

Some Pentecostals and Charismatics make the Holy Spirit the goal. No wonder some fundamental folks who consider soul-winning the goal sense that something is wrong. Instead of judging people for fighting the moving of the Holy Spirit, we Pentecostals need to be asking their forgiveness for making the gifts of the Spirit our goal. When fundamentalists rejected our wrong emphasis, they rejected the experience. If Pentecostals have power, then they should always be winning more souls than anyone else because that is what the Holy Spirit was sent to do—to make us witnesses for Jesus!

I can say with the Apostle Paul, I thank God that I speak in tongues (Corinthians 14:18, NIV). I pray in tongues so that I am supernaturally empowered to overcome the obstacles that try to stop me from winning thousands to Christ. Praying in tongues helps me to reach the goal. The same is true for all the gifts of the Spirit—they will help us to reach our goal but must never become the goal.

THE "INVERSION"

HOLY SPIRIT
"DEEPER LIFE"
SPIRITUAL GIFTS
PRAYER
FAITH
EDUCATION
PRAISE

SOULS

AN "INVERSION" OCCURS WHEN SOMETHING BECOMES THE GOAL OTHER THAN SOUL WINNING - DW

When an "inversion" takes place—that is when prayer or the gifts of the Holy Spirit are made the goal instead of being in their proper perspective as a means of reaching the goal—the church or the individual tends to move away from soul-winning and goes backwards. Soon, their ministries revolve in tight little circles, and they become more and more ingrown. Their churches experience little growth, if any; yet, they comfort themselves that they are "growing spiritually." Don't deceive yourself. If you are growing spiritually, you'll start influencing others to fall in love with Jesus. You'll win souls!

Right now, ask yourself: "Am I doing anything to win the lost?" If not, get down on your knees and ask forgiveness. Ask God to teach you how to win souls and to show you what he has for you to do. If you "thirst" for souls, God will satisfy that thirst. Begin today to do something to identify yourself as a soul-winner. Then, you'll be ready to enter another area of tremendous ministry—the ministry of intercession!

Low Risk Evangelism

One kind of evangelism has a very low risk of rejection. It's done in a group, so your fears are manageable. Best of all, people want to receive this kind of evangelism. It's called "Servant Evangelism" or "Show and Tell Evangelism."

Here's the idea. A group of Christians goes out into the neighborhood to rake leaves, shovel snow, wash cars, wash car windows, etc.—all for free. They say, "Hi. We're doing a community service project. May we wash your windshield? It's free." Permission is usually granted.

As the Christian begins to do the service, he says, "We're from such and such a church. We've been talking about the love of God a lot but figured we needed to show more of it. So we're doing this to show you God's love in a practical way."

People instantly agree that Christians have talked a lot about God's love but haven't done enough. They almost all think it's a great idea and gladly receive the service.

Show and Tell Evangelism shows them God's love before it tells them about it. As you show them love by wrapping their Christmas presents for free, or giving out free cans of pop at a football game, their hearts are opened. They ask questions. You can easily give them tracts—which they will read—because they are curious about any group that shows love in this way!

I first heard of this kind of evangelism from Ray Mayhew. Ray and his wife were one of two couples who started a ministry called ICHTHUS in London. Within about ten years it had grown to over 2,000 people with mid week meetings in 40 different locations throughout London. Ray's cell groups would go clean trash cans for free, wash windows in homes, etc., and display their joy and love through service projects. The results were phenomenal. After hearing this I still didn't grasp the Biblical principles deep in my spirit.

Two years later I read the book, *The Conspiracy of Kindness* by Steve Sjogren. His Vineyard Church in Cincinnati is one of the 25 fastest growing congregations in America. They do servant evangelism all over town and personally served 100,000 people in one year. They go to laundromats and put coins in the machines for people saying, "We just want to show you God's love in a practical way."

Every Christian can wash a car or clean windshields. When done as a group, it becomes a fun activity.

Because this kind of evangelism majors on showing love in kind deeds of service, the risk of rejection is very low. It also opens the heart before we try to reach the mind. Sinners love it. God blesses it mightily.

If Satan could give us a mental image of evangelism it would be, "Telling people what they don't want to hear." But Servant Evangelism is "Showing people what they want to see." People want to see God's love demonstrated to them in practical ways. There's a vast difference in these two mentalities.

The principles involved in Servant Evangelism are found in the teachings of Jesus.

He said, "Neither do people light a lamp and put it under a bowl. Instead they put it on its stand, and it gives light to everyone in the house. In the same way, let your light shine before men, that they may see your good deeds and praise your Father in heaven," (Matthew 5:15-16, NIV).

After washing his disciples feet as a servant, Christ said, "Do you understand what I have done for you? You call me 'Teacher' and 'Lord,' and rightly so, for that is what I am. Now that I, your Lord and Teacher, have washed your feet, you also should wash one another's feet. I have set you an example that you should do as I have done for you. I tell you the truth, no servant is greater than his master, nor is a messenger greater than the one who sent him. Now that

you know these things, you will be blessed if you do them,"
(John 13:12-17).

As Christians we are full of kindness and goodness. We have the nature of servants. If we "do these things"—serve people to show them God's love even as Christ did—we will be blessed! Whatever form of evangelism you use, get involved now.

Sam Couchran was praying when God gave him a vision of people from around the world in their native dress. They were crowded together and were reaching out toward a Bible suspended above them. They cried, "Give us the Book! Give us the Book!" But the Bible could not get to them. Then, in the vision, a trap door swung open beneath them and they fell down into the flames of hell. Sam could hear their screams and smell their burning flesh.

This vision was so profound Sam cried out to God, "Lord, you've got to give them the Book!"

The Lord told Sam, "You give them the book." God made it clear to him that it was his responsibility.

Is this clear to you? Do you realize you are entrusted with the Gospel and given the responsibility to spread it?

In response to this vision, Sam founded Light For The Lost, a layman's ministry within the Assemblies of God. As a result, Sam and the men who have embraced his vision have raised millions of dollars for Bibles and missionary literature. What are you doing to reach the lost?

An obedient person gets much better results from prayer than a disobedient person. Begin your life of prayer by laying a foundation stone of obedience to Christ's Great Commission. Soulwinners make the best intercessors.

2
THE PRAYER WEDGE

I was kneeling by the unconscious body of our senior pastor when God spoke to me, "You must pray daily for your pastor, or you're going to lose him."

My heart cried out to God, asking forgiveness for not praying for him sooner. He had preached a Sunday night message, walked a few feet into his office off the sanctuary, and collapsed. The crash as his two hundred pounds hit the floor brought people running and got people praying.

We prayed over him a long time before he was able to move. We rejoiced that he had not suffered a heart attack. But how long would it be until a time came when it really was too late to pray?

This was not the first time he had collapsed. On another occassion, the pastor had passed out behind the pulpit and been hospitalized for a time. It was easy to see that pressure and fatigue were draining the life out of him.

That night as I knelt by the pastor, the Holy Spirit prayed through me in a powerful way. I heard myself asking God to forgive the congregation for not bearing the pressure with Pastor, for letting him handle huge responsibilities and burdens alone, for being mere spectators as we watched him stagger under the load.

It was in this moment of crisis that I became conscious of a truth few laymen realize: pastors carry tremendous burdens. The better the Pastor—the more loving his heart is—the bigger that burden becomes. It was as if I could see our pastor carrying a huge mountain on his shoulder. It was far too heavy for him to carry, and it was crushing him. If I ran to help him, I, too, might be trapped under the weight of it because it was too big for two of us to hold up. But how could I let him die under that burden alone?

22

I vowed right then that I would pray daily for him, and I promised myself and God that I would do everything in my power to shoulder as much responsibility as I could to take some of the weight off of our pastor.

Lonely Under the Mountain

That night, I pondered my own fate. I was a Bible college graduate, ministering part-time at the church. God was directing me into full-time service, and I knew it. God was calling me "under the mountain," so to speak, to carry the burden of love for a lost and dying world. It had to be done. The world had to be saved. The responsibility had to be shouldered. Yet, I could see clearly that unless I could inspire lay people to shoulder the burden with me by prayer and by labor, the sheer weight of that responsibility would crush me, too, along with Pastor—and the church would lose both of us.

It's lonely under the mountain. That is not how God wants it. He says through Paul, "I want men everywhere to lift up holy hands in prayer, without anger or disputing," (1 Timothy 2:8, NIV).

We lift our hands to God to show our love as a child lifts his arms to his parents. But, upon those holy hands that are lifted up, God places the responsibility of winning the world to Christ, and there are not enough hands lifted up underneath it. Are yours?

"With all prayer and petition pray at all times in the Spirit, and with this in view, be on the alert with all perseverance and petition for all the saints, and pray on my behalf, that utterance may be given to me in the opening of my mouth, to make known with boldness the mystery of the Gospel," (Ephesians 6:18-19, NAS).

Oh, how I want to be an alert intercessor, ready at all times to stop the destruction of the church. I want to persevere in this—to never let down the guard but continually make intercession a way of life.

Notice this startling verse: "For we wanted to come to you—I Paul, more than once—and yet Satan thwarted us," (1 Thessalonians 2:18, NAS).

What? The great Apostle Paul thwarted by the devil? How could that be? How could a man who had all of the fruits of the Spirit and all nine gifts of the Holy Spirit operating in his ministry be thwarted by the devil? But that is what happened. The reason? Paul did not have enough people praying with him as he battled Satanic barriers in the spiritual realm.

Laymen tend to think of their pastors as such spiritual giants that they don't need prayer. Many times when I have asked people to pray for me, they give me a weird look, assume that I'm only asking for their prayers out of courtesy, and say, "Me pray for you? You pray for me!" Many Christians tend to see themselves as someone who needs the prayers of an anointed servant, a spiritual giant, not as someone called of God to assist a spiritual leader by adding the weight of their prayer support to his or her ministry. This tragic wrong thinking has killed many ministers before their time and has hindered the church in untold ways!

If any spiritual leader asks you for prayer, no matter how scrawny you are spiritually, pray as best you can. If you don't, you may be helping to kill him by draining his love, time, and prayers out of his life to help you, while giving no prayer support back. You are not being humble when you say, "Oh, no, sir—I need you to pray for me." You are just being plain stupid. Cut that nonsense out and start praying for your minister!

Paul wrote to a layman and said, "And one thing more: Prepare a guest room for me, because I hope to be restored to you in answer to your prayers," (Philemon 22, NIV). Your minister is hoping that you are praying for him. Don't disappoint him.

Splitting Satan's Barricade

Let me give an illustration that will help you understand what is happening in the spiritual realm where battles of faith are fought and won or lost. Let's say we are trying to get through a solid oak barricade. And, suppose we only have one big strong nail with which to split it. Picture in your mind this nail being driven into the oak, pulled out, driven in again over and over in an effort to split the wood. No matter how tough that nail is, it will bend and become unusable after awhile, and the oak barricade will just have a few nail holes.

Now, imagine a steel wedge being used to split the barricade. That wedge is not going to bend. If enough hammering is done, that oak barricade will split!

The spiritual application of this parable is this: the driving force behind the nail or the wedge is the compassion of God. The oak barricade is a Satanic barrier that holds souls in bondage. The nail is the pastor. God is desperate to get through that barricade to rescue lives. If the pastor is driven against this all alone, it will kill him.

OAK DOOR
(SATANIC BARRICADE)

ATTEMPTS FOR THE BIG BREAKTHROUGH

HARVEST REVIVAL

DRIVING FORCE
(God's Compelling Love)

NAIL *(PASTOR)*

ALL ALONE ONE MAN OF GOD MAY BE WORN OUT AND BREAK UNDER THE STRAIN - LIKE A BENT NAIL.

As 2 Corinthians 5:14, NIV explains: "For Christ's love compels us," [i.e., moves us with great force].

If a whole sack of nails were melted down and molded into a wedge, the wedge could do the job. In the same way,

IF YOU MELTED MANY NAILS DOWN AND FORMED A WEDGE YOU COULD SPLIT THE BARRICADE!! CHRISTIANS, LIKE NAILS, CAN BE MELTED TOGETHER BY GOD'S LOVE!

if the entire church puts their weight behind the pastor in prayer and labor, the pastor can still be the cutting edge—the leader—and not be destroyed. The barrier will be split and the victory won!

THE RESULT

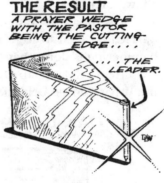

A PRAYER WEDGE WITH THE PASTOR BEING THE CUTTING-EDGE....

....THE LEADER.

What happens when people quarrel with each other, or get mad at the pastor? Satan takes away the strength from behind the pastor until he is left like a nail again. Do you see why loving one another is so important? Love is the fire that melts us all together into a wedge!

If we back God's man, there is going to be a split in Satan's barricade and a new opening of ministry will come.

THE BIG BREAKTHROUGH!

REVIVAL HARVEST

SATANIC BARRICADE

PRAYER WEDGE

GOD'S COMPELLING LOVE.

JUST AS A STEEL WEDGE AND HAMMER COULD SPLIT AN OAK DOOR, SO A PRAYER WEDGE AND GOD'S LOVE CAN SPLIT SATANIC BARRICADES!!

A great harvest will burst upon us!

"The God of peace will soon crush Satan under your feet," (Romans 16:20, NIV). Not under the pastor's feet alone, but under ours—the church's united effort in prayer! It will happen if we each do our part.

Moved To Action

In Acts 12:1-20 the Apostle James was killed, and Peter was to be executed. The church lost one great leader before it learned that apostles were only men and needed prayer backing. Convinced they would lose Peter, too, if they failed to pray, the church was moved to action before it was too late.

"So Peter was kept in prison, but prayer for him was being made fervently by the church of God," (Verse 5, NAS). The Bible doesn't say prayer was made for James. He died. It was made for Peter, and he lived to reap a great harvest.

Please note: James was one of the three men in Christ's inner circle. He was with Christ on the Mount of Transfiguration. He was trained for leadership. It was not God's will to have him die so young, or so early in his ministry. He went to heaven early because the church failed to take prayer seriously.

Many laymen have never been in real combat with the devil except in their personal affairs. But, they still want men of God to pray that they'll have the strength to win their private battle—and rightly so. They should ask for prayer.

Christians, however, need to remember that men of God are not just fighting with Satan in their private lives but are actually on the offense fighting him for the souls of millions of people. What a fight! What a job! What a responsibility!

If you could hear the voice of the great Apostle, there would be a tone in his voice that would send a chill up and down your spine as he cries out, "Finally, brothers, pray for us that the message of the Lord may spread rapidly and be honored, just as it was with you. And pray that we may be delivered from wicked and evil men, for not everyone has faith," (2 Thessalonians 3:1-2, NIV).

Shielded by Angels

In 1993 a young man asked God, "What does the prayer shield around Living Faith Church look like?" God showed Bob a vision of angels riding white horses. With no gaps between them, the horses followed head to tail behind one another until they formed a ring around our church. The angelic riders had swords upraised and were shouting praises to God. As the horses raced around the church, morale was high.

The vision continued, and Bob saw black horses with dark demonic riders coming to attack the church. They could not break through the ring of angelic protection.

The scene changed, and only one lone angelic horse and rider remained. His face looked grim, as if he would fight to the death against impossible odds. Bob heard only clip clop sounds as the horse walked slowly around the building. God said, "This is what the prayer shield looks like when prayer is neglected."

The scene changed again. This time the angelic horses and riders were all back racing around the church with no gaps between them. God spoke, "This is what the prayer cover should/could look like." The words "should" and "could" were spoken at the same time.

While these angelic riders raced around the church, a wall of holy fire shot up around the building. It was as tall as the building and about three feet thick. If any enemy penetrated the first line of defense they would run into the wall of holy fire!

Then eight giant angels appeared between the ring of fire and the church building. They were so huge their swords were as long as our building was tall. Just one of them could wipe out the demonic riders that had appeared earlier. If any enemy made it through the angelic riders and through the wall of fire, they would be destroyed by these mighty angels.

> **Our angelic guard is no better than our combined prayers for our church. This is why intercession is so tremendously important.**

By praying loving prayers for your pastor or other authority figures, you are laying an important stone in your foundation for prayer. That stone is called "submission to authority". There is no better way to submit to those in authority than to pray diligently for them.

Kenneth Hagin once had a vision in which Christ told him that at the Judgment many Christians would be shocked to find God held them personally responsible for President Richard Nixon's failures. Why? Because they had not prayed for him.

Vietnam veteran Roger Helle wrote a book about his experiences in the Vietnam War titled "Point Man." As the point man, Roger had to go in front of his company of troops and find the snipers, booby-traps, and other dangers. It was the most dangerous of assignments. Roger was shot and bayoneted, but he lived by a miracle of God.

Pastors are point men. They are out front—and are the main target of the enemy. Always respect them for this. Honor your spiritual leaders and don't shoot them in the back with criticism, gossip, and slander. Keep them covered in prayer. You could be held responsible for the mistakes they make when they don't have adequate prayer cover. So don't judge them. Judge yourself.

Are you praying enough for your leaders?

3
FORGIVE BEFORE
THEY ASK

One day when I was a volunteer choir director and not yet on staff, I was severely reprimanded by an important deacon right in front of my choir. I had done nothing wrong, and it was obvious to all who witnessed this incident that he was acting very immaturely.

Realizing how wrong he was, I graciously told the Lord, "I'll forgive him, God, just as soon as he asks forgiveness."

Meanwhile, I carried around a lot of resentment toward him. Whenever I would see him, I'd think about what he had done, and a churning feeling would come into my stomach. I was bitter.

I remembered the scripture that says, "If your brother sins against you, rebuke him. If he repents, forgive him," (Luke 17:3, my paraphrase). With this verse, I justified the anger and bitterness in my own heart by telling myself: "If he repents, I'll be gracious and forgive." But he didn't repent.

Days went by. He acted perfectly normal, as if nothing had happened. I wasn't forgetting, and I wasn't happy. The sweet peace of the Holy Spirit seemed to leave me whenever I'd think about this incident or see this man.

Finally, when I was in prayer, the Holy Spirit revealed to me what I was like. He gave me this illustration to show me how silly I was being. It may sound carnal, but it has helped me greatly, and it is from God.

The Dirty Bird

A man was walking down by the ocean when a sea gull flew over his head and dropped "do-do." It landed on the gentleman's nose.

THE SEAGULL ILLUSTRATION: WHY BEING BITTER IS STUPID.

YOU DIRTY BIRD YOU! I'M GOING TO LEAVE THIS RIGHT HERE ON MY NOSE UNTIL YOU COME BACK AND WIPE IT OFF!!

LESSON: SOME PEOPLE WILL DO SOMETHING DIRTY TO YOU AND FLY AWAY LIKE A BIRD. THEY MAY NOT EVEN REALIZE HOW THEY HURT YOU. IT WAS JUST A NORMAL DAY FOR THEM!

Highly indignant, the man yelled at the bird, "You dirty bird, you! I'm going to leave this right here on my nose until you come back and wipe it off!" The bird flew on, and the man returned home.

The next day at work, people began to snicker at the large white blob of stuff on this man's nose. Not only did people notice it, but the man himself was aware of it every moment, and it made vision difficult. Once in awhile, he'd go outside to see if the bird was flying around.

Days went by. Finally, he began to think, "I've waited for days now, and that bird hasn't come back to wipe this off. I'm getting awfully tired of it. He might never come back. I think I'll just wipe if off myself."

He did and felt a great deal of relief. His friends thought he looked a lot better, and he could see better, too!

The Lord told me, "You are like that man. Bitterness is showing on your face. The deacon may never come back and apologize. Others

NEXT DAY AT WORK:

PEOPLE ARE NOTICING THIS FUNNY STUFF ON MY NOSE!!

LESSON: BITTERNESS SHOWS ON YOUR FACE AND YOU CAN'T HIDE IT.

are noticing that you are bitter because you can't hide its results. It's blocking your spiritual vision, also. Why don't you just forgive the man before he asks and be free?"

What a revolutionary idea! I had to decide if it was worth it. Many people prefer keeping their anger stirred up.

LESSON: WAITING UNTIL SOMEONE ASKS FORGIVENESS IS DANGEROUS. YOU COULD CARRY BITTERNESS ON YOUR FACE THE REST OF YOUR LIFE.

But, I was tired of not feeling the sweet presence of the Lord. Besides, that man might be a "bird" and never come back to make things right.

That settled it. "Lord," I prayed, "I really do forgive this man with all my heart. I'm not going to bitterly remember this incident anymore." I was free! What a tremendous lesson!

Jesus prayed, "Father, forgive them, for they know not what they do," (Luke 23:34, KJV). At the time Jesus prayed that, his enemies were taunting him, saying, "If you are the son of God, come down from the cross." Others were parting his garments among themselves. No one was asking forgiveness! If he had been bitter—and he had plenty of reasons to be—he would have sinned, and we would not have had a perfect Savior.

THERE, I WIPED IT OFF MYSELF! WOW!! I FEEL AND LOOK BETTER!

LESSON: YOU CAN FORGIVE PEOPLE BEFORE THEY ASK FORGIVENESS AND BE FREE FROM BITTERNESS!! (WHY WAIT?)

But, he overcame the last temptation, the temptation to be bitter.

This lesson was so liberating to my spirit, I got in a habit of forgiving people before they asked. Whenever I

JESUS FORGAVE WHEN NO ONE WAS ASKING FORGIVENESS

FATHER, FORGIVE THEM.

was wronged, I would forgive them and then pray that God would bless them. Then, I would immediately feel happy inside.

The Bible says, "The cheerful heart has a continual feast," (Proverbs 15:15, NIV). It is better to be having a feast in your heart than to let bitterness be eating you up!

Got Someone Under Your Skin?

The Bible says, "See to it that no one misses the grace of God, and that no bitter root grows up to cause trouble and defile many," (Hebrews 12:15, NIV). A "root of bitterness" takes hold when a person is wounded by someone and he doesn't forgive.

Bitterness is like a sliver. If you got a sliver in your arm, and you didn't pull it out, it would start to fester. In a few days, your arm would be really sore. In a few weeks, it could be swelled to twice its size, and blood poisoning could be setting in. Anyone who lightly bumped that swollen arm would send terrible pain through your body. You would react. You would accuse him of hurting you. Perhaps you would even hit him back and wound him.

Bitterness produces the same results. It gets down under your skin and hurts. The longer it is there, the worse it gets. Because of its irritation, you think others are hurting you when they really are doing things quite innocent and harmless. Bitter people who feel pain as someone lightly brushes that swollen part react in anger and strike back. They call names. They get revenge. In short, they wound other people, and then others have a root of bitterness in them. Unless they pull it out, it will fester; and when someone bumps them, they'll react in bitterness and wound someone else. Can you see why a root of bitterness can defile *many?*

Cleaning the Files

If you are still bitter about something that happened to you in your childhood, or at the last church you attended, etc., why not forgive the people who wronged you? Even if they are dead, you need to forgive them. Otherwise, the memory of their evil actions is living in you, and bitterness is feeding on you. Instead of a merry heart that is having a feast, bitterness is feasting on you. Certainly, a dead person can't come back to ask forgiveness. So why let that dead person ruin the rest of your life?

Use the chorus of a song I wrote to check your bitterness level right now.

"Do you think about the past in hurt and anger?
Then your future is as dark as it can be.
For the problem isn't others, it's in you, oh, can't you see?
If you'd pull that sliver out, your wound would heal, and you'd be free."

The most peaceful feeling will come to you when you forgive those old hurts. Most people keep a mental file of everything anyone does wrong to them. When someone does something wrong again, the little card pops up, and they react in anger against all the wrongs done to them by that person over a twenty-year period.

This is especially true in marriages. Many marriages end in failure because husbands and wives are keeping a record of wrongs. With each new wrong, the hurt is greater, and the reaction to it is meaner and more violent.

The Bible says in 1 Corinthians 13:5 (NIV): "Love keeps no records of wrongs."

Do you want a love-filled marriage? How about destroying the card file you've been keeping all these years? Don't keep those old records of wrongs any longer.

God's Pliers

THE ROOT OF BITTERNESS ILLUSTRATION: WHILE TRYING TO CATCH A SICK CALF I FELL DOWN. HE DRUG ME THROUGH A CACTUS.

One time I was working with my dad on his cattle ranch in South Dakota. We had to catch a sick calf and give him a pill. Since calves can run so fast, I got on the running board of our old truck. Dad drove up by the calf when he wasn't suspecting anything, and then I jumped off and grabbed him by the tail. As soon as I could slow him down, I was going to grab his leg and throw him to the ground.

Instead, the calf pulled me downhill, and jerked me off my feet. I thought, "I'll hang on and get his leg when he slows down." But when he drug me through a big cactus, I let go.

THOSE LONG SPINES HAD TO BE PULLED OUT IMMEDIATELY OR THEY WOULD HAVE FESTERED. I COULD HAVE GOTTEN BLOOD POISONING, LOST MY ARM, OR DIED. I PULLED THEM OUT AS FAST AS I COULD.

My shoulder had about twenty big, long cactus spines stuck in it, and I was bleeding. My dad immediately got the pliers and began to pull the spines out. They were pushed in so deep that we couldn't pull them out with our fingers. But there was only one thing to do—get them out of my shoulder immediately. Although my arm was sore for a couple of days, I was okay.

Suppose I had said, "No, I just can't pull them out. I'm never going to pull them out." I would no doubt be dead by now from blood poisoning.

IF A SLIVER (ROOT OF BITTERESS) IS NOT PULLED OUT (FORGIVEN) YOU'LL SOON HAVE A PAINFUL, SWOLLEN ARM (WOUNDED SPIRIT). IF SOMEONE BUMPS THIS ARM (SLIGHTLY OFFENDS YOU) IT WILL FEEL LIKE YOU'VE BEEN HIT WITH A SLEDGE HAMMER.

Bitterness has to be dealt with as soon as you feel it jab into you. Even if it's hard to forgive, get your Heavenly Father's pliers (extra power to forgive) and pull those old slivers of bitterness out.

Jesus said, "And when you stand praying, if you hold anything against anyone, forgive him, so that your Father in heaven may forgive your sins," (Mark 11:25, NIV). If we have bitterness in our hearts, our prayers won't be answered.

In 1 Peter 3:7, God tells husbands to "be considerate" of their wives so that their prayers won't be hindered. Being inconsiderate of people hinders prayers just as bitterness does. We could do a lot to improve our prayer life if we would be kind and loving to everyone and forgive all who wrong us, forgiving them immediately, even before they ask forgiveness.

WHY DOES EVERYONE HURT ME? EVERYONE IS MEAN TO ME! LIFE IS HORRIBLE!

BUT I JUST BARELY BUMPED HIM. HE HAD NO REASON TO EXPLODE THAT WAY!

HE SHOULD HAVE PULLED IT OUT WHEN IT HAPPENED.

This lesson is vital for anyone who wants God to use him in the ministry of intercession. Intercessors are never bitter. They continually cleanse themselves from the contamination of bitterness.

The Apostle Paul is a good example. He was a real soul winner and a true intercessor. He wrote, "When we are cursed, we bless...when we are slandered, we answer kindly," (1 Corinthians 4:12-13, NIV). That's one of the keys to the life of this great man of God. Bitterness never robbed him of his anointing!

As a person grows in the grace and knowledge of God and the Lord Jesus, it becomes possible to be so quick to forgive that bitterness can't take hold even for a second. You literally become encased in "the armor of God." (See Ephesians 6:11.)

Look at how quick Paul was to forgive. Someone would say to Paul, "I curse you." Paul would immediately say, "I bless you." The bitterness didn't even penetrate! What a key to a Spirit-filled victorious Christian life!

Keep yourself cleansed from bitterness by having a loving heart that is so fast to forgive that it blesses those who hurt you by reflex !

FORGIVE—THEN FORGET!

The lesson of "forgiving before they ask" was far more vital to my survival in the ministry than I realized.

After serving as an associate pastor for five years, I traveled as an evangelist. After eighteen months of that, I moved to Omaha, Nebraska, to pioneer a new church. Becoming the Senior Pastor was an adventure in pain. I became the main target of demonic forces that sought to ruin the church.

People did the cruelest things to me. All pastors can match stories of agonizing emotional pain caused by the people we love. Without the ability to forgive, I'd have disappeared down a black hole of bitterness.

The meanest trick of all was played by people who would give demonic prophecies, saying God would destroy our church because I was a "bribe taker" or some other equally absurd and slanderous charge. I'd forgive, then go on in spite of all the garbage that had been heaped upon me. But often I'd review the incredible amount of insults and abuses I had suffered.

In my heart I'd say, "I forgive them, Lord, but they sure treated me terribly. I've probably been mistreated more than any pastor in history." Then once again I'd review the long list of painful memories.

One evening in a revival service, the lady evangelist who was our guest speaker came up to me and quietly said, "Wes, the Holy Spirit tells me that you are holding something in your hand, and it's hindering your work. The Lord wants you to let it go."

LESSON: YOU GET BITTERNESS OFF YOUR FACE BY FORGIVING. YOU GET SELF PITY OUT OF YOUR HAND BY FORGETTING. YOU CAN'T FOCUS ON JESUS IF YOU DON'T FORGET WHAT YOU'VE FORGIVEN.

"What is it?" I asked.

"The Lord won't tell me. He's going to tell you," she said.

I went home that night and asked the Lord what I was holding in my hand that was hindering my work. The answer was startling. IT WAS BIRD POOP! I'd been wiping it off of my face by forgiving people, but then holding it in my hand.

God let me know that I was continually opening my hand to look at the filth that had been dumped on me—and feeling sorry for myself as a result. It wasn't enough to just forgive and get the poop off my face. I had to FORGET IT in order to get it out of my hand.

So once again, I chose to turn at the Lord's correction. I made a decision not to focus on the wrongs done to me. I'd wipe each wrong off my face by forgiveness and wash my hands of it by forgetting it.

The Bible says, "Forgive whatever grievances you may have against one another. Forgive as the Lord forgave you," (Col. 3:13 NIV).

LESSON: YOUR WORK FOR GOD WILL PROGRESS RAPIDLY WHEN YOU FORGIVE AND FORGET!

There is a proper way to forgive—as the Lord forgave. And how does he forgive? He forgets your sin! He remembers it no more. He removes it as far as the east is from the west . . . out of sight and out of mind. That's the way we all need to forget the awful things people have done to us.

The devil really doesn't care if you forgive as long as you don't forget. Why? Because either way, you'll be looking at bird poop. If you don't forgive, it's on your face blocking your vision. If you don't forget, you'll be opening your hand to keep looking at what you wiped off your face. Either way, your focus won't be on Christ.

Living for God's Approval

After this experience, God taught me one other powerful lesson so I could enjoy the ministry and not have my heart broken over and over.

I was jittery and worried about what people thought of me. Would they love me tomorrow? Would they leave the church? What were they thinking about me? Had their opinion of me changed? The devil was driving me nuts with these kind of thoughts.

Then the Holy Spirit taught me not to be concerned about others' opinions because I would not have to answer at the judgment for what *they* thought. I would only have to answer for what *I* thought. My thoughts were the ones I needed to be concerned about.

39

The Bible says, "Though rulers sit together and slander me, your servant will meditate on your decrees," (Psalm 119:23 NIV). The worst person to be talking bad about you is a ruler—one with influence! The worst thing he could say is slanderous lies! But even if that is happening, we must choose to NOT think about what they are saying, but choose to think how we can practice the Word of God.

Is your enemy hungry? Feed him! Is he thirsty? Give him something to drink. Pray for him! Bless him! Turn the other cheek. Go the extra mile. (See Romans 12:20, Matt. 5:38-41, I Peter 3:9.) Verses that tell us how to respond to our enemies with love should be our focus. If we think on these verses and DO them, then we are good and can enjoy the approval of God.

The hardest times for me were when I began to believe I was as bad as people were saying I was. When I insulted myself, life became unbearable. But I've learned to "take no lip off the devil."

Never agree with a spirit of condemnation. You are good if you are a doer of the Word. Live for the approval of God and know in your heart who and what you are. Be content with that.

You may never be able to change someone's opinion about you, and you could wear yourself out fretting about it. Or, you can do as I have learned to do: Concentrate on what you think of them. Think loving, kind, forgiving, intercessory thoughts and prayers. Then you can rest in the approval of your God.

4
HOW TO BE A
PEOPLE-PERFECTOR

Learning to never be bitter helped me immensely. But often, I was critical. I would talk about peoples' problems with others and often would be able to identify what was wrong with them. It would even be "the truth." But, I never felt good about it afterwards. There was always an unclean feeling that lingered whenever I would talk about someone.

Once when I was in Texas, I was washing my face at the motel where we were staying. I thought I didn't get the soap off my face, so I rinsed it again. It felt coated and sticky. Finally, I realized it was the water. There were so many minerals in it they stuck to my skin. It felt terrible! In fact, being dirty felt better than washing. It was impossible to drink, and it stunk besides. The people in that area had to import their drinking water. I'll never forget trying to rub that water off my face.

That is how it is with gossip. Even when it is true, it leaves a sticky feeling. You can think it's as pure as water, but there are things in it that will pollute you. And it stinks!

God wants us to be part of the solution. Anytime we just talk about people without going on into loving intercessory prayer, we are not being part of the solution. You can be one hundred percent right and be critical.

A critical spirit makes you wrong. A critical spirit has the same effect as bitterness. It ruins your prayer life. God wants to speak to you, but when you are critical, it cuts off communication with God.

Accuser or Intercessor?

Many people do not understand what it means not to be critical. It is not just thinking everyone is okay. Everyone is not okay. Some people have terrible problems. An intercessor will know those problems and be completely aware of them. But an intercessor reacts differently than the person who gossips.

This is easy to understand when you compare how Satan and Jesus react to people's faults. Satan is continually accusing people. "For the accuser of our brothers, who accuses them before our God day and night, has been hurled down," (Revelation 12:10, NIV). That verse means that the Apostle John saw a vision of the day when Satan would be thrown down, but as yet he is still accusing us day and night.

Jesus, on the other hand, is interceding continually for us. "Therefore, he is able to save completely those who come to God through him, because he always lives to intercede for them," (Hebrews 7:25, NIV).

A good example of this is found in Luke 22:31, NIV: "Simon, Simon, Satan has asked to sift you as wheat. But I have prayed for you, Simon, that your faith may not fail. And when you have turned back, strengthen your brothers."

Jesus knew Simon was weak, and told him that he would deny him three times. Satan knew Simon was weak, also. They reacted to this knowledge in completely different ways. Satan asks permission to totally destroy Simon. Jesus went into loving intercession and saved the day. One verse of a song I have written highlights this point:

"Now Jesus could gossip of all our sins,
and all our faults reveal,
like the devil who accuses day and night,
and comes to destroy, kill, and steal.
But instead, he is our advocate
and intercedes in prayer.

Since he lives in our heart,
we all ought to start
to act like he does up there!"

Most Christians will say "Amen" to that, but few are really in the habit of intercession. It needs to be a reflex or a habit. If it isn't, you'll be slipping back into accusing people.

Many Christians when they talk to God sound more like the devil than Jesus. "God," they pray, "you know what so and so did? You see that terrible thing he has done? God, you're not going to let him get away with that, are you?"

God says, "Honey, the devil is reminding me that I'll have to judge him, and he has already told me everything you're telling me."

How sad when we sound and act like the devil and think we are spiritual.

Just because you are "spiritual" enough to know when someone is in the wrong or to know when someone has a wrong attitude doesn't mean a great deal. What counts is what you do with that information. Do you become critical—or do you go into loving intercession?

That is so true, I want to repeat it a bit to make sure you understand. When a person does get close to the Lord, it is easier to see when others are wrong. But, if we start condemning them, then we ourselves have fallen into sin because we didn't go into intercession. Criticism is a "natural reaction" of the flesh. But, we have to learn to react in the Spirit.

This lesson is called "basic intercession." Many people feel they have a ministry in prayer, and they will pray for hours. Then, they'll get up and butcher people with their tongue, and think they are very spiritual.

God would rather hear a tired soul-winner pray one sentence than to hear hours of prayer from a self-righteous gossip.

What Is Basic Intercession?

Most people are failing at "basic intercession". In football, if you have all the razzle-dazzle plays, and yet you are not good at the basics—such as how to make a tackle and how to throw a block—you'll be a losing team. Christians think of intercession as something far out—as when Moses prayed on the mountain for forty days without food or water in the presence of God, interceding for Israel.

Or, they visualize intercession as being when the Holy Spirit would wake them up in the night with a vision of some missionary about to be killed and eaten by the cannibals, and high-powered intercession is needed to save his life. But that is not basic intercession. Unless you get the basics down, you'll only touch on intercession from time to time, but you won't be an intercessor. You won't live the life. You won't continually stand in that ministry.

What is basic intercession? It's when you see a fault in a Christian and go right to prayer. From God's great storehouse of character qualities, you take whatever that person needs and begin to "pray it" into his life.

Example: Suppose a person is easily influenced to sin, and he is in and out with God. What does he need? The intercessor figures this out before he or she prays. The person wavering in his relationship with God needs "steadfastness."

Many Christians are shocked at the idea that it is possible to pray a character quality into someone's life. But we see great Bible intercessors doing this all the time.

Notice the Apostle Paul's prayer for the Philippians. "This is my prayer: that your love may abound more and more in knowledge and depth of insight, so that you may be able to discern what is best and may be pure and blameless until the day of Christ, filled with the fruit of righteousness that comes through Jesus Christ, to the glory and praise of God," (Philippians 1:9-11, NIV).

Look closely at this scripture. Paul is taking character qualities out of the vastness of God's storehouse, and in intercession is moving these characteristics toward the Philippians. His prayer of basic intercession is moving love, knowledge, insight, and discernment into their lives.

If Paul were a gossip or a critical person, he could have put it this way: "You guys just don't have enough love!

There are a lot of things you don't know, either! Your insight into spiritual things is just not what it should be! Sometimes, you don't even know the difference between right and wrong—you don't discern what is best all the time. I'll bet pretty soon you commit some sin, and then you'll bring a lot of reproach on God's name."

Do you see how Paul could have used his ability to see a lack of spirituality in people's lives in a way that would have been condemning?

This is the way many Christians react when they see a fellow believer with a fault. Instead of praying the needed character quality into his or her life, they point out the fault and consider themselves to be spiritual and discerning. They tell God about it, and even worse, they tell other people, which is just what the devil wants them to do.

Getting Rid of the Gungies

Intercessors have to train themselves to react like Christ when a fault is noticed in a fellow believer. The minute a character fault is noticed, they must figure out what the opposite of that is. If, instead of doing this, they look at the fault and talk about it, they get a good case of what I call the "gungies." This is a spiritual condition that would be similar to wading in mud and then letting it dry between the toes. Perhaps the mud feels good—but after it dries, it feels "gungie". Let me give a personal example.

While doing a Sunday School bus route, I was accompanied by a converted alcoholic. This man had been gloriously saved and filled with the Spirit. I had taught him about soul-winning and intercession, and we were out signing up bus kids together. As we passed a particular church, old memories came to mind.

"You know," I said to my friend, "I like almost everybody in the world but the pastor of that church. He is one of the few people I just can't stand. One time, he chased one of our church ladies around a bed. He's a woman chaser and an immoral man, and he calls himself a minister. I just can't stand that guy."

We drove on, and then my partner—the new convert—said to me, "You know, Wes, I've heard you preach better before."

Have you ever been caught not practicing what you preach? Well, I really felt gungie. I pulled the car over and said, "You're right, Pat. We're not going any further until we figure out what that man needs, and we pray for him."

We really had to think. That was a hard one. Finally, we decided a big dose of self-control would help him. So I prayed. First, I had to ask God to forgive me for being part of the problem and for being a bad example to my friend. Then, we prayed earnestly for God to give the man a spirit of repentance and self-control, and to save his soul from hell. The Spirit returned, and the "gungies" left.

Right now in your mind, you may think of people you just can't stand. Is that any excuse not to love them or pray for them? What do they need? If you aren't doing something about it, you have become part of the problem, and that critical attitude will rob you of prayer power. It cuts off the communication line that comes from heaven to your soul. It stops the flow of divine communication.

Train yourself. If you know their fault, then it should not be too difficult to figure out the opposite of that and pray it into their lives. Are they full of doubt? They need knowledge of the scriptures to fill them with faith. Are they stupid? They need wisdom. Are they irritable all the time? Patience should fix that up. Are they lazy? Ask God to help them be diligent. On and on we could go.

Praying Down Blessing

After you have figured out what would be a definite help to the person, you are ready to approach God. Be sure to make a loving prayer. We pray because we love. Asking God to break someone's leg or to get him in a car wreck to teach him a lesson and to get his attention, is not the way to pray. That is not a loving prayer. That is a prayer of judgment.

Some Christians unwittingly practice witchcraft by praying prayers to God that only demons would want to answer.

A demon would rather work evil for a Christian than work evil for a witch. Be extremely careful of angry prayers.

God's great storehouse of wonderful character qualities is always open. Get a whole cartload of these. In other words, don't just ask God to do one nice thing, but rather pray the most wonderful blessing possible down on the person. As you start praying, a sweet peace will flood your soul. This kind of praying does as much for the one who prays as it does for the recipient of the prayers. You'll make yourself a new person by praying these kinds of sweet prayers.

Few things are as sickening as a Christian who knows everyone's faults and haughtily displays a "holier than thou" attitude. What if you have a critical attitude hindering your spiritual life? When you begin to pray for the other person, your prayers will clean out your own spiritual channel first! You actually bless yourself!

On the other hand, when you condemn and criticize, the first person you injure is yourself. You cut off the blessing of God on your own life the minute you cut another person down with your tongue.

"Do not judge, or you too will be judged. For in the same way you judge others, you will be judged, and with the measure you use, it will be measured to you," (Matthew 7:1-2, NIV).

Psalms 109:17-18 (NIV) says: "He loved to pronounce a curse—may it come on him; he found no pleasure in blessing—may it be far from him. He wore cursing as his garment; it entered into his body like water, into his bones like oil."

These verses contain a tremendous truth: what we say about others will affect our lives! If we say negative things—gossip and critical talk and cursing—it will come back on us and enter into us, affecting our whole lives. Since this is true, let us be careful to make loving prayers for people, prayers that would bring blessing to them. Then these kind things we have spoken will enter our body like water and our bones like oil. We will have blessed ourselves.

Just take a minute to pray a loving prayer for some minister or layman, and immediately a sweet sense of God's presence will enter into you. Since our words about others will affect us, let's be careful to build others up by prayer so that we ourselves will be blessed.

Expose or Cover?

The next step in basic intercession is to get your mind on the answer to your prayer and off the problem. "Visualize" the person you are praying for as completed. If he is irritable, visualize him as being patient. Don't expect him to be irritable when you see him again. Expect a change.

If you saw a man who had a huge ink blot on his shirt, your eyes would immediately shift down and stare at that ink blot. Bad character qualities in people's lives are just that way. They attract attention, but the intercessor refuses to look at them.

Instead, an intercessor will take a character quality from God and hold it out toward the needy person. The big

49

"blot" is covered up by the gift. The eyes of the intercessor see no fault. They are looking at the character quality they are praying into the life of the person in need.

This is what the Apostle Paul was talking about when he said, "Finally, brothers, whatever is true, whatever is noble, whatever is right, whatever is pure, whatever is lovely, whatever is admirable—if anything is excellent or praiseworthy, think about such things," (Philippians 4:8, NIV).

An intercessor must control his or her thought life. We must not allow ourselves to meditate on other people's shortcomings or upon our own. We must have our eyes squarely on what we're praying into people's lives and look at that. Think on that. Meditate on that. Dream about that. Love them as if they were already that way.

The Bible says, "He who covers over an offense promotes love, but whoever repeats the matter separates close friends," (Proverbs 17:9, NIV). Certainly this doesn't mean to cover over your own sins because the Bible says, "He who conceals his sins does not prosper, but whoever confesses and renounces them finds mercy," (Proverbs 28:13).

It means to cover over other people's faults and failures with loving intercession, asking God to place wonderful traits

THE EYES OF THE INTERCESSOR SEE NO FAULT—THEY ARE LOOKING AT THE CHARACTER QUALITY THEY ARE PRAYING INTO HIS LIFE.

in place of the shortcomings. Can you see how this promotes love?

Proverbs 10:12 (NIV) says, "Hatred stirs up dissension, but love covers over all wrongs." Love covers wrongs not by ignoring them, or sweeping them under a rug, so to speak, but covers them with prayers of loving intercession.

A vivid picture of this is given to us in Genesis 9:20-27. Noah got drunk and was lying naked in his tent. His son, Ham, came in, saw his father's fault and shortcoming, but did nothing about it. He did not cover it.

Instead, he walked out and began to tell others about it. Those he told, Noah's other two sons, reacted the way an intercessor does. "But Shem and Japheth took a garment and laid it across their shoulders, then they walked in backward and covered their father's nakedness. Their faces were turned the other way so that they would not see their father's nakedness," (v. 23, NIV).

This is what the intercessor does: he covers over wrongs and shortcomings. And the intercessor is careful not to look at people's faults. They look at people only after they have covered them with a beautiful garment of prayer.

When Noah awoke, the spirit of prophecy came upon him. By the gift of faith he pronounced God's curse upon the descendants of his youngest son who had looked upon his nakedness. These people became the Canaanites who were later uprooted from the land. They were also the people who lived in Sodom and Gomorrah. The curse was a real curse of divine judgment.

It is a fearful thing to look at people's faults and then talk about them. You'll bring trouble to yourself and your family if you do that!

Noah, also by the Spirit of God, pronounced a blessing on those who had covered him, and they were blessed.

Devouring One Another

It is impossible for Satan to stop the church. The only force that can stop the church is the church. That's why Satan likes to get church people finding fault with one another, and he has succeeded to a remarkable degree because we have played along with him. "If you keep on biting and devouring each other, watch out or you will be destroyed by each other," (Galatians 5:15).

Jesus said in Luke 10:19 (NIV): "I have given you authority to trample on snakes and scorpions, and to overcome all the power of the enemy; nothing will harm you."

Nothing from the devil can stop the church. But the church can kill itself. Let us dedicate ourselves to the ministry of intercession so that we become people perfectors instead of flaw inspectors. "Our prayer is for your perfection," (2 Corinthians 13:9, NIV).

Let's promote love. Let's be peacemakers. Let's be the sweet spirits that bind the church together so tightly in love that no division can get started, and then let's steamroll over the devil together.

In Bible college, we would have nightly devotions at our dormitory. Often, these would degenerate into fierce arguments about certain hair-splitting questions. We all had a reason why we were mad. One night, a converted hippy kid jumped to his feet, and in a look of amazement at our stupidity, exclaimed, "Why can't we all just love one another?"

All of the reasons we may have had for fussing and squabbling seemed so immature, so stupid in the face of that simple question—Why can't we just love one another?

Developing Spiritual Immunity

From time to time "waves" of criticism go through a church, very similar to an outbreak of influenza but in the spiritual realm.

In 1981, I pioneered a new church in Omaha, and one year later, an old, established church merged with us. Mergers are always difficult, but to make matters worse, I hired some staff members I shouldn't have. It seemed that every one who made an appointment to see me was telling me why they were leaving the church.

During this time we had a revival meeting led by two women evangelists. One night, they said the service couldn't progress unless people asked forgiveness of each other and got things right.

Several came to me to say they had been critical, but the last one stunned me. He was the sweetest, most loyal man in the church. When he said, "Please forgive me. I've been critical of you," I readily forgave. But then I left the service in a black cloud of despair.

The devil began to speak to me. "It's hopeless. You don't have a chance. I can make anyone critical of you—even the sweetest man in the church. You can stack up your blocks, but I'll just kick them down, and there's nothing you can do."

At that moment, the devil seemed bigger than God. I went to bed feeling sorrowful and defeated.

The next morning, while I was still in bed, God spoke to me. He reminded me of an experience I had when I was a boy. My two sisters and I were each given a kitten by our elderly neighbor who lived on the cattle ranch next to ours.

"These two kittens will probably die of distemper," she warned. "But this kitten will probably live. You see, this kitten's mother caught distemper and nearly died. But she overcame the disease and lived and has probably passed an immunity on to her kitten."

It happened just that way. Two kittens caught the dreaded disease and died, while the other one grew up healthy and happy. As God reminded me of that experience, he said, "This man caught the disease, but he didn't die. Now he's gained an immunity to a critical spirit and can pass that immunity on to his spiritual kittens."

A great new courage flooded into me—and I knew God was bigger than the devil. I also knew that Satan takes a great risk whenever he tries to make someone critical.

Many times Satan wins because the infected ones infect others, and all of them fail to grow into healthy, mature Christians. Many actually die spiritually of this disease, backsliding away from God.

But not everyone dies! Not everyone stays critical. Some overcome it as the Spirit of God deals with their hearts. And as they turn at God's correction, a strong immunity is built into them, one which can be passed on to those they disciple. If that happens, Satan's ploy backfires, and he finds his efforts to infect the church have only caused it to become stronger.

If you would like to be immunized <u>before</u> you catch the spiritual disease of a critical spirit, (a demonic viewpoint) then go through the Word of God and collect "sweet spirit verses." A list of these is printed in the back of this book. There are immunities in these verses. Memorize them and practice them. Collect other verses the Holy Spirit shows you.

If you have been critical, repent, and begin to practice "basic intercession." Be a pastor backer, not a pastor attacker. Be a people perfector, not a flaw inspector. And remember, the very first person you'll bless with this improved attitude will be yourself! "A kind man benefits himself," (Proverbs 11:17 NIV).

5
LEARNING THE SECRET OF POSSESSIVE LOVE

A certain layman in the church where I served as an associate pastor didn't like me. I was sure of it. I could tell by the way he acted that he had something against me—or so I imagined. Whether real or imagined, I'm still not sure. But, since I thought he didn't like me, I decided I really didn't like him very much either.

One day, the Lord started to deal with my heart about brother so and so. As the Spirit dealt with me, I suddenly said to my wife, "You know, I'll bet if I picked up old brother so and so on my Sunday School bus, I'd love him."

That hit me really hard. It was true. No matter how big the troublemakers were who rode my bus, they counted in my bus total. They were mine. I was trying to win them to Christ. I worked hard at keeping them coming.

God was teaching me a real lesson. Why did I love those kids who were such problems, yet dislike a born-again brother who was not a very big problem at all? Why would I fight so hard to keep from losing a problem child, and not care if brother so and so ever came back? I thought about this for many days.

I remembered Donnie and Ronnie. They were identical twin boys who rode my wife's bus to church. They were like cartoon characters in that when you set them down, their legs were spinning before they hit the ground; and when they did, they took off like a cartoon character does on TV. And both in different directions!

One day, an usher was trying to catch one of them. One little fellow dived into the church office. The usher was after him. The kid went under a table, then stuck his head out and bit the usher in the leg. And then, he called the usher a very nasty six letter word! The usher was ready to bite a nail in half.

The senior pastor, the children's pastor, and the board member who was the usher, all told me we'd have to stop picking up Donnie and Ronnie on the bus.

It was my duty to inform my wife. But when I did, she started bawling. Drop Donnie and Ronnie? Unthinkable. Something had to be done. So my wife, Bonnie, would take Ronnie by the hand and sit with him in the four-year-old room while Donnie was put in the three-year-old room. As soon as the teacher had Ronnie's attention, Bonnie would go into the three-year-old room and help control Donnie.

This went on for many weeks. It was exhausting, but then the boys' mother started coming to church, and soon made a profession of faith in Christ. Possessive love had paid off.

Nobody else cared enough about Donnie and Ronnie to put up with all that hassle. But they "belonged" to my wife in that she had signed them up, visited them every week on the bus route, and counted them in her bus total. They were "her bus kids." Someone else's bus kids might be too big of a problem, but no problem seemed too great to keep her own kids from coming. They were hers. And that demanded a special love.

What if I picked up the entire church on my bus, I thought. I bet I would have a new love and affection for each one. They would be "mine"—not someone else's. No matter how big of a problem they were, I would still love them. Then, scriptures started to come to mind, and God started to communicate with me.

All Thine Are Mine

The words of Jesus as he prayed in John 17 came forcibly to my mind: "Father, all thine are mine," (verse 10, KJV).

"That's the way I want you to feel, Wes," God seemed to be saying to me. "Love all my people as if they were your very own converts."

"Even the pastor, Lord?"

"Yes, even the pastor."

I was beginning to see something about intercession I'd never seen before. There is a love that will not let go of a person. It is not a domineering, bossy love laced with selfishness, but it is the kind of love Paul felt when he said, "I am jealous for you with a godly jealousy. I promised you to one husband, to Christ, so that I might present you as a pure virgin to him," (2 Corinthians 11:2, NIV).

Because of this love Paul felt, he just could not let the Corinthians go into false doctrine. They were his. His possessive love demanded something extra from him. His possessive love for the Galatians moved him to write, "My little children, of whom I travail in birth again until Christ be formed in you," (Galatians 4:19, KJV). His great, possessive love was the

FATHER, ALL THINE ARE MINE.

key to being able to move into mighty intercession and travail of spirit to save an entire church from apostasy.

God wants us to move into possessive love. When we do we are getting really close to the deeper lessons of intercession. Travail in the Spirit must surely be the next step.

Let us love each other, then, as if we all were each other's converts. A new convert is like your baby, with all kinds of questions and problems. But you gladly put up with him and help him learn to cope because he belongs to you—if you led him to Christ. We must begin to see that we all belong to each other because we all are a part of each other. We have a perfect right to say with Jesus, "Father, all thine are mine."

Let us be very careful not to say to one brother who has a fault, "We don't need you," and to one who has a weakness, "We can get along better if you'd leave." Remember the words of the apostle Peter, "Now that you have purified yourselves by obeying the truth so that you have sincere love for your brothers, love one another deeply, from the heart," (1 Peter 1:22, NIV).

6
SURGICAL LOVE

Throughout this book, when I refer to being "critical," I mean people who have the "devil's point of view". We do not want to speak, think, or act according to the devil's point of view. But we must speak, think, and act from God's point of view.

If Christians get into *idolatry* or *rebellion,* their sin must *NOT* be covered. It must be bravely and boldly exposed, even at the risk or loss of your life. *God will never cover rebellion or idolatry.*

Nathan didn't cover David's sin. He exposed it. David had rebelled against the Word of the Lord by committing adultery, deception, and murder. He was not repenting. This meant he had moved out from under the atoning cover of the blood covenant, and God's holy eyes saw his sin! If he died in that condition, he would go to hell. So Nathan applied what I call "surgical love."

We are saved by grace, not works. Since we cannot earn salvation by good works some say, "Therefore we cannot lose salvation by evil works." Their oversimplification misses a clear focus of truth. We *do* have to do something to be saved—repent and believe. The opposite of repentance is rebellion, and the opposite of faith in God is idolatry. Two things get you into Christ—-repentance and faith in God. Two things can get you out of Christ—rebellion and idolatry—faith in a false god.

Surgical love has to operate to get out a cancer of idolatrous or rebellious sin. It was this type of love Jesus showed to the Pharisees.

Two creatures I know of strip bark from trees—the porcupine and the woodpecker. The porcupine is destructive because it eats live healthy bark and kills living trees.

The woodpecker only strips off dead bark which is infected with insects that could kill the rest of the tree—or the rest of the forest!

In the same way, attacking people who are "under the blood," those whom God sees as "holy in his sight without blemish and free from accusation" (Col. 1:22 NIV) is wrong! That's destructive—like the porcupine. But attacking the rot and filth of rebellion or idolatry is really a life-giving kindness—like the woodpecker!

Surgical love will sometimes "drill" into a person. To the undiscerning, this appears rude and unloving. But to the knowledgeable, it appears as a kindness of absolute necessity.

The Spiritual Surgeon

I've learned over the years that God uses the sweetest, most loving people as vessels through which to pour out his rebuke and judgment.

Take John the Beloved. He always wrote about love. Such a sweet guy—the one who leaned back upon our Lord's breast and heard the very heart beat of the Savior. Yet John was God's choice when he needed a prophet to rebuke rebellion and idolatry in the church.

Christ, in Revelation Chapters 2 and 3, as recorded by John, rebukes five of seven churches, then orders the churches to read each other's "mail." This was really the most loving act Christ could have done.

Moses was the meekest man on earth. Yet when he saw the golden calf, he burned with anger (God's anger at sin), burned the idol in the fire, ground it to powder and then threw it on the water and made the people drink it! He did this to totally desecrate the idol, making it pass through their digestive tracts and come out in their feces. Thus, if they wanted their detestable idol back, they would have to pick through their filth to retrieve it!

Practice forgiving love, perfecting love, covering love, and possessive love. Fill every day from top to bottom with kindness. As you do this, you will mature to the place God could use you to perform "surgery." But acting as a spiritual surgeon carries a high responsibility and you must be very, very sure there is no plank in your own eye. If there is, you'll kill your patient!

One Sunday evening a few of our church members performed a skit called "Dr. Ungentle." We had him operate for cancer (in silhouette). He opened his patient up with a power saw, then dynamited the tumor, and blew his patient up totally. He walked out from behind the silhouette with blood (ketchup) all over himself and said, "I did it! I did it! I got ALL the cancer! " True, but he killed the patient in the process. (Then he was arrested for murder.)

Only the humble will ever be able to "operate" in surgical love. Others may try it, but they'll not have the discernment it takes and will dismember, maim, or kill their patient.

I cannot stress this strongly enough! Walk humbly with your God. I would advise you NOT to try to operate in this kind of love unless you are highly skilled in the other types of love first. Remember, "Man's anger does not bring about the righteous life that God desires," (James 1:20 NIV). This means—it won't bring about a righteous life in the person you rebuke because your words will be man's anger, devoid of God's love.

To Kill or Cure

Once I preached a sermon on hope. I explained that hope is what you see in your mind, and faith is what you believe in your heart. Hope and faith work together. Faith is of the spirit realm, while hope is in the soulish realm. Hope works like the guidance system of a rocket, while faith is like the rocket engine. While I preached this, one man in our church drifted away into other thoughts. Later he wrote me a letter correcting me.

The day I got his letter, I was very tired and was already dealing with lots of stress. His letter talked down to me and from it I could tell he had not even listened to my sermon. He was arguing that hope is what God lays up for us in heaven and that my definition was all wrong.

I decided he needed a rebuke of wisdom! I wrote one that steamed. Then I tore it up. I wrote another. I tore it up, too.

DR. UNGENTLE OPERATES FOR CANCER WITH DYNAMITE...

THIS CANCER HAS GOT TO GO! WHAT AN AWFUL THING!!

LESSON: HUMAN ANGER CANNOT WORK THE RIGHTEOUSNESS OF GOD. ONLY PERFORM SURGERY IN GOD'S ANGER.

I DID IT!! I GOT ALL THE CANCER!

KABOOM!

LESSON: GOD'S ANGER HATES SIN-BUT LOVES THE SINNER. HUMAN ANGER HATES SIN AND THE SINNER AND DESTROYS THE PATIENT. THIS IS CRIMINAL!

I wrote a third one, and it sounded as mean as the first two. This time I said in my heart, "Well, this must be the Spirit of God because that's all that will come out." I mailed the letter.

Then I drove to a Minister's Institute, a weekend retreat for pastors. I could hardly keep my mind on the services, wondering what would happen when the man in my church opened and read that letter. I prayed, I cried, and prayed some more. Then God spoke to me.

"Do you want to <u>kill</u> him or <u>cure</u> him?" God said. "I want to KILL him!" I answered honestly. Then I repented in tears and said, "No God, I really don't want to kill him. I <u>really</u> want to <u>cure</u> him!"

God continued, "He is thinking of hope the noun. You are talking about hope the verb. Explain that to him, and he'll understand your sermon."

So I called him and said, "Brother, I wrote you a letter in a wrong spirit. Whatever you do, don't open it. God has spoken to me and when I return, we'll get together and work things out."

When I returned home, I met with the man, explained my sermon again with what God had told me. He agreed with my explanation of hope completely then. But I shudder to think what would have happened if he had opened my letter bomb. I would have blown him to shreds emotionally, and like "Doctor Ungentle," I could have bragged, "I got all the cancer." Thanks be to God who delivered me from blood guilt!

The next time you are ready to apply surgical love, ask yourself this little question, "Do I want to kill or cure?" If you detect mere human anger and irritation—DON'T OPERATE! <u>Your anger won't work righteousness. Your anger hates the sinner. God's anger hates the sin.</u> That's why we must move in his anger from time to time— but never our own.

THE WAY IT SHOULD BE:

THANKS, I NEEDED THAT!

IT TOOK 8 HOURS IN SURGERY, LOTS OF CAREFUL TENDER WORK, BUT WE GOT THE CANCER—AND YOU'RE GOING TO RECOVER FULLY!

I repeat: God's anger hates sin. It operates and goes after the destructive tumors of rebellion and idolatry to destroy them and SAVE the patient. Man's anger hates the sinner and solves the tumor problem by blowing them up along with the patient!

May God use you in surgical love because it is very much in need in our society. And may God deliver you from the blood guilt caused by mere human anger.

7
THE RESULTS OF
THIS LIFE

The Bible says, "A happy heart makes the face cheerful," (Proverbs 15:13, NIV). Also, "The cheerful heart has a continual feast," (Proverbs 15:15, NIV). Life really takes on a new brightness when you live a life of intercession. I have so much to learn about intercession, but what I have learned has made my life wonderful.

Most people are continually hindered by bitterness and critical attitudes. They have to try hard to have fun to cover up the pain of bitterness or the "gungie" feeling of a critical spirit. The intercessor, however, is completely free of these—that is, the one who is living the lifestyle of a real intercessor. It is a continual feast. There is a continual joy. There is an abiding peace. Problems brought on by circumstances don't look so big. The way out seems clear. Prayer becomes easy. In fact, it becomes continual.

Paul wrote, "Be joyful always; pray continually," (1 Thessalonians 5:16-17, NIV). What did he mean by "pray continually"? I believe he meant to keep your spirit so free from contamination that you are feasting in your spirit all day. You are constantly communicating with God until your thoughts and his thoughts begin to merge, and you begin to live in "the mind of Christ," (1 Corinthians 2:16).

If you will forgive those who have hurt you, intercede for others who have faults, and never think about those faults, but think on the good things you are praying into those lives, you'll feel like a brand new person.

Another advantage to living the life of an intercessor is that it becomes easy to hear from God. Many people pray for hours trying to hear from God. They beg God to speak. Heaven is silent. Or is it?

Perhaps God is literally shouting at us, desperately trying to communicate, but our spiritual line of communication is jammed with bitterness, critical attitudes and thoughts. God likes to talk to his kids! If you'll do your part to keep your spiritual channel to heaven clear of contamination, I can guarantee you'll hear the "still small voice" (1 Kings 19:12) speaking to your spirit.

Hearing From God

When my heart is clean and I'm loving everyone, praying blessings down on others and especially on those who have visible faults, I hear from God no matter where I am or what I'm doing. For instance, God uses me to write songs. These songs start coming, and I don't have to be in prayer to get them. But my "channel" has to be clear. I wrote the song, "I Like Obeying You," while I painted a garage. The song "The Unclean Can Always Touch Jesus" came to me while I was trying to purchase a CB radio for a bus. And, there are many other instances of this.

THE SWEET SPIRIT OF AN INTERCESSOR IS A GREAT CONDUCTOR FOR GOD'S VOICE.

I HEAR YOU LOUD AND CLEAR, LORD.

Once while mowing the lawn, God spoke to me so many things regarding my future ministry and how to go about it, that I had to keep stopping and writing down what he was telling me. The roar of the lawn mower didn't keep me from hearing that "still small voice" because God speaks to our spirits. A bitter spirit, however, will hinder that voice from getting through.

I love to hear God speak. Nothing on earth is as great a delight as hearing his voice. The only thing that is more fun is obeying his voice.

Seeing Through the Master's Eyes

It might be said that the life of an intercessor helps you to have good "spiritual ears"—that is, you can hear what God is saying. But another wonderful advantage is that the intercessor develops good eyes, eyes like the Master's which see potential in people that others would overlook.

Let me tell you a fable that has been helpful to me in the ministry. A huge lion catches a tiny mouse under his paw. He is about to squish the little mouse, but the mouse begs for his life, assuring him, "I'll pay you back some day for this kindness." The lion scoffs at that idea. What could a lowly mouse do for the "King of the Jungle"? But, he let the mouse go anyway. A few days later, the lion is caught in a huge rope snare. He roars and roars but cannot get free. The mouse rushes to his aid, gnaws the ropes in two and releases the lion just before the hunters get there.

In the church, there are people who seem to be about as worthless as a mouse. But, I've learned not to overlook anyone. You never know who will be your real friend when you need one.

As an intercessor, I began to see potential in people. In fact, many times the person I was seeing it in did not see it himself. Then, God began to let me see through his eyes. That is one of the ways I was able to get a staff of workers for Oregon's largest bus ministry. I looked at each person who came in as a possible answer to my prayer for workers. Even when I was dealing with lost people, I would often visualize ministries in them.

I remember one couple who were parents on my bus route. They seemed so nice. I could visualize them taking my bus route over, even though they weren't serving God. But soon, they did come to church and dedicated their lives to Christ. I gave them some tapes of bus seminars, and sure enough, they decided to take over my route for me and did an excellent job.

The Bible says that David's army of men consisted of men whose "potential" was hidden to the natural eye. "All those who were in distress or in debt or discontented gathered around him, and he became their leader. About four hundred men were with him," (1 Samuel 22:2, NIV). His army consisted of the rag-tags, the culls of society, the "they'll never amount to anything" type of people.

God anointed David with his Spirit and made David a dynamic leader. He was able to take these men, and by God's help, some were transformed into the mightiest men the world has ever known. There were thirty-seven men in this army who did supernatural feats equivalent to Samson's. They were invincible under God's anointing (2 Samuel 23:29).

ONE PERSON AS SEEN BY TWO PEOPLE

MR. WORTHLESS

MR. USEFUL

HE'S UNTRAINED AND A NEW CONVERT. HE WON'T BE ANY HELP. I WISH GOD WOULD SEND OUR CHURCH SOME WORKERS.

WOW! WHAT A PRIZE! HE'S GOING TO BE A REAL SOULWINNER. I CAN SEE SO MUCH POTENTIAL. THANKS FOR MY MIRACLE, GOD!

Mighty men are usually not mighty to begin with. They are usually "in distress or in debt or discontented." They have to be developed. Don't expect them to be imported into your church. They must be raised up.

An intercessor will be able to look at the average layman and see a mighty man through the eyes of Jesus. If your church needs mighty men and women of God to do the work of the ministry, someone will have to have the eyes of Jesus that will enable him to look at a common layman and see a mighty man.

This is not hard for an intercessor. They pray for workers and find them. They pray for workers and develop them. An intercessor helps turn the common into the mighty. They are people perfectors, not flaw inspectors.

Blessing Conscious

There is a third advantage to a life of intercession. When your spirit is right before God, each problem that comes your way can be converted into a blessing.

God wants his people to become "blessing conscious", not "trial conscious." When a problem is overcome, it is then a blessing. It is a testimony!

Problems are just opportunities for an intercessor because if one's spirit is right, the problem will have to convert into a blessing.

Few people live this kind of an overcoming life because they are failing in the areas of loyalty and love. This will take another chapter to discuss in detail.

8
TURNING PROBLEMS INTO BLESSINGS

When your spirit is right, God has a way of turning every problem you encounter into a blessing. God wants his people "blessing conscious" not "trial conscious."

John 1:16 (NIV) says, "From the fullness of his grace we have all received one blessing after another." This doesn't just happen by accident.

There are at least four areas in your life that dictate whether a problem stays a problem, or if it is converted into a blessing.

The four things that will keep a problem being a problem are: 1) unbelief, 2) disobedience, 3) bitterness, and 4) a critical spirit. If your life is free from contamination in these areas, all problems will convert into blessings for you.

This means you'll have to be a person who has the opposite character qualities in your life: 1) faith, 2) obedience, 3) forgiving spirit, and 4) loving intercession for others. You can see that the intercessor will have the jump on other people as far as blessings are concerned. They'll be way out ahead in areas 3 and 4. But all intercessors might as well go all the way with God and master areas 1 and 2 as well.

First, let's look at some scriptural instances where problems were converted to blessings.

Joshua and the Jordan River

Moses had died and Joshua was Israel's new leader. This was a staggering responsibility because the Israelites were a very difficult people to govern.

God told Joshua to lead the people into the promised land, but right away a big problem was encountered: the Jordan River at flood stage (Joshua 3:15).

Most followers of God would react in this manner: "Oh, no! Look at that river! How are we going to get across that? We'll all drown for sure! Who got us in this mess anyway? What are we going to do now?" These people look at a problem and don't visualize how it can convert into a blessing.

They should react like this: "Wow! That's a big problem! It's going to be a whopper of a blessing when that thing converts over! This is going to be exciting! All right, God, what is your plan for this miracle?"

The plan God gave to Joshua has much significance for us. "And Joshua said to the people, 'Sanctify yourselves [that is, separate yourselves for a special holy purpose], for tomorrow the Lord will do wonders among you!'" (Joshua 3:5, Amplified).

You'll notice that before the problem was turned into a blessing, the people had to do something. They had to "sanctify" themselves. Sanctify means, among other things, "to purify or free from sin." When this was done, God gave the plan. The plan was followed, and the waters of the river stopped flowing and piled up in a heap, (Joshua 3:16).

That was a blessing! They knew God was with them for sure, and that no enemy was going to have a chance against his mighty power. Joshua was firmly established as God's man because God had used him to achieve the miracle. Thus, it was a special blessing to Joshua because it allowed God to supernaturally confirm his divine appointment as their leader.

"The Lord said to Joshua, 'This day I will begin to magnify you in the sight of all Israel, so they may know that, as I was with Moses, so I will be with you,'" (Joshua 3:7, Amplified).

Paul and the Hurricane

God was taking Paul to Rome to have him testify to Caesar. Satan didn't want this great man of God to get to Rome and was determined to stop Paul. Paul, however, was free of unbelief, disobedience, bitterness and a critical spirit.

God warned Paul that the voyage would be made at great loss and danger (Acts 27:10). Satan worked hard on the ship's owner, the pilot, and the Roman Centurion who was in charge. They didn't listen to Paul.

As the ship set sail, Paul knew he was in grave danger. A big problem was on the way, and he couldn't do anything to stop it. But, he sanctified himself. He went to prayer.

Sure enough, such a huge storm enveloped the ship that it was driven in the wind for days, and all hope of being saved was given up by the crew. On the thirteenth night of the storm, an angel of God appeared to Paul and told him the plan. The ship would run aground on an island, and if all stayed in the ship, they would be saved.

Paul relayed this message, and it happened exactly as he said. Since he had declared what was going to happen in the future twice to them, they believed Paul was a mighty man of God! Not only were their lives spared, but it seems that many, if not all of the crew, were converted to Christ. The problem had converted to a blessing with many men finding Christ.

Satan doesn't give up easily, however. Someone once said to an intercessor, "You always have something good to say about everyone. I'll bet you could even think of something good about the devil!"

The intercessor thought for a moment and then grinned, "Well, he is a hard worker."

Such was the case when Paul and the crew landed on the island. Satan was ready to strike with another problem.

Paul and the Snake Bite

Since it was rainy and cold on this island, the sailors built a fire. Paul naturally got right in and worked with the rest of the men.

While he was putting a big armload of brush on the fire, a poisonous viper came out of the branches he was carrying and bit him on the hand. The snake was fastened to Paul's hand with its fangs stuck in his flesh. It hung there twisting and writhing until Paul was able to shake it off into the fire.

That's what God wants us to do with problems. Shake them off!

The natives expected Paul to swell up and die immediately. So did Satan. He had thrown his best shot at the man of God. But Paul's spirit was completely right with God. He was filled with faith. He was in total obedience!

When he didn't die, the natives thought he was some kind of a god. Now, they were more than willing to believe anything Paul said.

As a result, his fame spread over the island, and more people came to believe in Christ. Another problem had converted to a blessing. (Story found in Acts 28:1-6).

Paul and the Deadly Fever

Satan was really angered by now. Two great problems had turned into blessings for Paul. The enemy decided to try again. (It's fun to live for God in such a way that if Satan leaves you alone, you'll win the world, and if he attacks you, you'll win it quicker!)

A fever struck the people of the island. It was accompanied with dysentery.

One of the first to be afflicted was the father of the head man of the island. I'm sure Satan hoped it would wipe everyone out, and especially Paul. But Paul walked right into the presence of the sick man and showed no fear that he, himself, would contract the deadly disease. Paul laid his hands on the man's fevered brow, and Christ healed the man! Then, everyone on the island who was sick began to come to Paul, and they were healed. The entire island received the good news about Jesus!

Paul and the Problem of Chains

To most preachers, being bound in chains would present a real problem. But, any problem can convert to a blessing if you position yourself properly.

The "judo technique" involves using the weight and power of your opponent to throw him. We can do this in the spiritual realm with Satan. We must position ourselves under the blood of Jesus, fill ourselves with the Word, instantly obey, be quick to forgive, and always pray for others.

How do you suppose this problem is going to become a blessing to Paul?

"Now I want you to know, brothers, that what has happened to me has really served to advance the Gospel. As a result, it has become clear throughout the whole palace guard and to everyone else that I am in chains for Christ. Because of my chains, most of the brothers in the Lord have been encouraged to speak the Word of God more courageously and fearlessly," (Philippians 1:12-14, NIV).

Satan thought some chains would keep the Gospel from having a bigger foothold in Rome. Instead, the Gospel sent tremors through the entire palace guard and went right to the top of government leadership. Paul couldn't have gotten the Gospel to these people with human planning. It was a tremendous blessing for him in his endeavor to spread the good news of Christ!

That is why Paul could write, "And we know that God causes all things to work together for good to those who love God, to those who are called according to his purpose," (Romans 8:28, NAS).

Problems—God's Opportunities

Many downtrodden Christians quote this verse and comfort themselves a little with it. Somehow, they believe their poverty, sickness, loneliness and a host of other problems are working for their good.

Be careful here. Problems aren't blessings. They are problems. They must be converted to blessings. They must be overcome before they become blessings.

You must never just thank God for the problem and keep it. That is capitulating to the devil. Don't leave your problems unconverted. Sanctify yourself. Set yourself to seek God and his plan to turn obstacles into blessings.

The Bible says, "A righteous man may have many troubles but the Lord delivers him from them all," (Psalms 34:19, NIV). I would like to paraphrase that verse this way, "The righteous will encounter many problems, but the Lord will turn each one into an experience of deliverance and blessing!"

God isn't sending these problems. Many of them are caused by adverse situations and circumstances. Some are caused by people and some by direct attacks of Satan. But, God is not the source of the problem—he is the source of the deliverance! "He [Jesus] became the source of eternal salvation for all who obey him . . ." (Hebrews 4:9, NIV).

I trust that the Holy Spirit will make this real to you! God wants you to be blessed all the time. Problems are just opportunities for God to demonstrate his love for you. In

Deuteronomy 28, God says to those in his covenant: "If you fully obey the Lord your God and carefully follow all his commands I give you today, the Lord your God will set you high above all the nations on earth. All these blessings will come upon you and accompany you if you obey the Lord your God. You will be blessed in the city and blessed in the country. The fruit of your womb will be blessed, and the crops of your land and the young of your livestock, the calves of your herds and the lambs of your flocks. Your basket and your kneading trough will be blessed. You will be blessed when you come in and blessed when you go out. The Lord will grant that the enemies who rise up against you will be defeated before you. They will come at you from one direction but flee from you in seven. The Lord will send a blessing on your barns and on everything you put your hand to. The Lord will establish you as his holy people, as he promised you on oath, if you keep the commands of the Lord your God and walk in his ways. Then all the peoples on earth will see that you are called by the name of the Lord, and they will fear you. The Lord will grant you abundant prosperity—in the fruit of your womb, the young of your livestock and the crops of your ground— in the land he swore to your forefathers to give you. The Lord will open the heavens, the storehouse of his bounty, to send rain on your land in season and to bless all the work of your hands. You will lend to many nations but will borrow from none. The Lord will make you the head, not the tail. If you pay attention to the commands of the Lord your God that I give you this day and carefully follow them, you will always be at the top, never at the bottom. Do not turn aside from any of the commands I give you today, to the right or to the left, following other gods and serving them," (Deuteronomy 28:1-14, NIV).

You will notice in this wonderful passage that when enemies come at one who is in the blood covenant with God, their defeat is predetermined! They'll flee from you in seven ways! This is the way it is with problems. When the devil sends a problem, it can turn into seven different blessings. Can you see why God wants his people blessing conscious?

Are You Qualified for Blessings?

There are qualifications for blessings. First, you have to have faith in the blood covenant. Faith in the blood! If you are under the blood, you are under the blessings.

Galatians 3:13-14 (NIV) is the New Testament bridge that allows us to cross back into the Old Testament and possess Abraham's blessings: "Christ redeemed us from the curse of the law by becoming a curse for us, for it is written: Cursed is everyone who is hung on a tree. He redeemed us in order that the blessings given to Abraham might come to the Gentiles through Christ Jesus, so that by faith we might receive the promise of the Spirit."

Put your faith in Christ's atoning work for you. You are a candidate for blessings because of his blood, not because of any good deeds of your own. Learn your covenant rights. Then, begin to possess them.

"Faith comes by hearing, and hearing by the Word of Christ," (Romans 10:17, NKJV). Get into the Word. Get all the faith you can.

If you are ignorant of the scriptures that produce faith, you won't be able to have faith. It's the Word of God's responsibility to produce faith in you. It's your responsibility to read the Word, and then meditate on it until it goes from your head into your spirit. That is where the Word produces faith. It begins to let off divine energy for miracles! So do everything you can to get rid of all unbelief.

There are many good books being written today on the subject of faith. The best book of all is the Bible—so tank up on scriptures! There is so much faith in each verse. Your problem can stand only so much faith, then the problem will have to convert to a blessing. So fill up on scriptures!

If you are lazy in this and just hope you'll be accidentally blessed, problems will come to your life and they'll stay problems because of your lack of faith. God's Word tells you how to get faith: swallow the Word! The Word will produce faith if you'll get the Word inside you. How much faith you get is entirely up to you. If you want a lot, then dive into the Bible.

Obeying God's Plan

The second qualification for continual blessings is obedience. Jesus said, "If you love me, you will obey what I command," (John 14:15, NIV).

This ties in perfectly with Romans 8:28 (NAS): "And we know that God causes all things to work together for good to those who love God". If you don't obey God, you really don't love him. And, if you don't really love him, you don't qualify for having every problem turn into a blessing. Problems that come to you when you are in disobedience will stay problems until you repent!

Let me give you a miracle formula:

A NEED (a problem) + GOD'S PLAN
+ OBEDIENCE = A MIRACLE (a blessing)

When some monstrous problem comes, get in touch with God immediately! He has just the plan that will cause it to be converted to a blessing. Then, do exactly what his plan says. God will only bless his own plans. Don't plan your way out of a problem and ask God to bless that. He won't bless your plans. He only blesses his own.

You'll see this little formula at work throughout the Bible. When the wine ran out at the wedding feast, that was a big problem. They got in touch with Jesus, and he told them a simple plan that sounded stupid.

"Jesus said to the servants, 'Fill the jars with water'; so they filled them to the brim. Then he told them, 'Now draw some out and take it to the master of the banquet.' They did so, and the master of the banquet tasted the water that

77

had been turned into wine. He did not realize where it had come from, though the servants who had drawn the water knew. Then he called the bridegroom aside and said, 'Everyone brings out the choice wine first and then the cheaper wine after the guests have had too much to drink, but you have saved the best till now,'" (John 2:7-10, NIV).

God's Word is filled with instances where men encounter big problems and God gives them what appears to be a stupid plan. How is it going to help Moses to get more than 600,000 Jews across the Red Sea by just holding his staff out over the water? Yet, it worked and that problem, when it was overcome, was a tremendous blessing that made the women sing and dance for joy!

"I Can't Believe It!"

Many times when something goes wrong, Christian people will say, "That figures!" Then, when something goes really good they say, "I can't believe it!" Their words reveal a condition of unbelief in their hearts.

God has taught me to change those words around. When something really good happens, I say, "That figures." Why? Because I'm under the blood of Jesus, and that means I'm under the blessing. I'll be blessed when I'm in the city, and blessed when I'm in the country! I'll be blessed coming in and blessed going out. Since I'm always either in the country or in the city, coming or going, I am always under the blessing! God said he'd make me the head and not the tail, and that I'd always be at the top and never at the bottom (Deut. 28:1-14). So, it figures that things should go well with me. God wants us to expect blessings!

When something goes wrong, it surprises me and I say, "I can't believe it." And in fact, I don't believe it! I have learned better. Let me give an example.

My wife and I were on a tour to the Midwest for evangelistic meetings. At one stop she took out a suitcase to get something for the baby, but she didn't put it back in correctly. As I pulled the car up, it fell out the back window of our station wagon. We didn't miss it until we were 700 miles away. It contained over $100 worth of things—our camera, her electric curlers, the baby's vitamins, a tape recorder, etc.

I said to myself, "I can't believe it. This doesn't look like a blessing." It just seemed so odd. I'd come to expect blessings—not problems. I didn't even pray about it, but I did think that losing $100 worth of stuff was no blessing, and I did expect something really good to happen.

It did. That figures! Someone found the suitcase, turned it in to the police in Missoula, Montana, and my uncle who lives there retrieved it. Nothing was missing! They shipped it back to us for $3.00. While in Iowa, a lady gave my wife a set of electric curlers, and then we had two sets!

Converted Problems

Let me give another example. While in Spokane, Washington, preaching at a meeting, a friend needed me to fly to Eugene Oregon to preach the funeral service for his mother. I got up at 5:00 a.m., flew to Eugene, preached the message and flew to Pasco. I changed clothes, shaved, and was ready to fly to Spokane to preach my closing service of the meeting. But the airport at Spokane fogged in! I was stranded in Pasco. My flight was canceled, and I did not want to spend any money on a motel. It looked like a real problem.

I phoned my wife and told her to tell Pastor Everett Olp that I would not be able to get there. Satan reminded me that I'd lose an offering and the money from book sales. It looked like this would be a financial disaster for me. I was really wanting to preach my message, too, and the thought of not getting to close the meeting properly was unbearable. When the problem (the fog) didn't go away, I knew God would turn it into a blessing. That figures! Here is how it happened.

One of the men who had planned to fly from Pasco to Spokane spoke up and said, "I'm going to rent a car." Two other men and I asked him if we could ride along and split the rental. Our refund on our plane ticket was $43, and the car rental was $16 each. So I made $27 there.

We got to Spokane around 9:30 p.m.—too late for my meeting, but I didn't have to wait up all night in a motel lobby. Instead, I ate a late supper with my wife and baby and got a good night's sleep in our lovely motel. The pastor had taken an offering for me although I wasn't there, and my wife had sold $78 worth of books and tapes.

GOOD NEWS — I CAN'T BELIEVE IT!
BAD NEWS — THAT FIGURES
PEOPLE WITH UNBELIEF IN THEIR LIFE CAN'T BELIEVE IT WHEN GOOD THINGS HAPPEN—BUT BELIEVE READILY IF SOMETHING SOUNDS BAD.

GOOD NEWS — THAT FIGURES
BAD NEWS — I DON'T BELIEVE IT. IT HAS TO TURN INTO A BLESSING.
PEOPLE WHO HAVE FAITH ARE NOT SURPRISED AT GOOD NEWS. THEY EXPRESS DISBELIEF IF THINGS SOUND BAD AND EXPECT GOD TO MAKE ALL THINGS WORK FOR THEIR GOOD.

Besides that, they held me over another day, so I got to preach my message. The next day I enlisted twenty-two children to ride their church bus, then I preached that evening to a good crowd. The problem had been converted to a wonderful blessing.

When problems come to Christians, the natural reaction is to pray, "Lord, make this problem go away." That is what the disciples did when people began to faint from hunger after following Jesus in the wilderness for three days. They said, in effect, "Lord, we've got a problem here. People are so hungry, you had better send them away so they can get food." (Please send the problem away, Lord.)

But Jesus had other plans—namely turning the problem into one of the greatest miracles in the New Testament. He told the disciples to have the people sit down, and then He fed five thousand with just a little boy's lunch!

Moses reacted the same way at the Red Sea. He wished that it wasn't there so he could flee from the army. But the sea was there so that God could drown Pharaoh's army in it!

One day our neighbor took a chain saw, cut all the branches off the cedar trees on his side of the boundary, and then came around on my side and cut off all the branches there. The trees had been a beautiful hedge of privacy, but he cut them off from the ground up about six feet on five trees before his wife stopped him.

I was sick. But I didn't say, "That figures!" I said, "I can't believe it!" What kind of a blessing could God bring out of butchered trees?

I had used up $5000 making a song book and had run out of money. I needed $729 worth of paper to print the first thousand books. Our neighbor's homeowner's insurance covered the damage he had done to my property, and the bill was $747. So, I bought all the paper with it.

Now God didn't make this man cut down my trees. I believe the devil did that. But God turned it into a blessing.

God has a plan for all the problems you will encounter. He will deliver you out of them all! But remember Joshua's words, "Sanctify yourselves."

Sanctify means "to purify or free from sin." If you have been unbelieving, ask forgiveness and then strengthen your faith by feeding on God's Word. If you have been disobedient, repent and obey. If you have been bitter, forgive. If you have been critical, intercede! Then God will give you the plan. All you will need to do is obey the plan!

Sometimes, you will just have to trust because God sees things that you can't see. But take your stand and believe that only blessings can come to your life! Command those problems to convert into blessings in Jesus' name. If God gives you a specific plan to make this happen, instantly obey.

9
BEWARE OF
INTERNAL PROBLEMS

In the preceding chapter, we gave Bible evidence that all problems can be converted into blessings. All the problems mentioned had one thing in common: they were external. However, there is such a thing as an internal problem, and these are the ones that are especially dangerous.

One night when I was a young associate pastor, it fell my lot to turn out all the lights in the church and lock up. As I remember, I was working extra late and by the time I got ready to lock up, it was totally dark outside, and I was all alone in the building.

As I was going down into the basement of the church to check all the lights and doors, the thought came to me, "What if the devil jumps out from around the next corner?" Just the thought of that scared me a little. Then I remembered, "Greater is he that is in you than he that is in the world," (1 John 4:4, KJV). However, when I went back upstairs and sat down at my desk, I was still wondering what it would be like if the devil suddenly jumped out to scare me.

As this thought lingered in my mind, an alley cat walked underneath the window behind me, and let out the most chilling "meeeooooooowwwwwww" I've ever heard. It made the hair on my neck stand up, I'm sure. I jumped in fright.

Just then, the Lord spoke to my spirit. This is what he seemed to communicate to me: "Wes, don't ever be afraid of evil forces when they are outside of you. If they were to jump out in front of you, they would be no trouble for you to handle. Be afraid of them only when you allow evil forces-—evil attitudes and thoughts—-to come inside of you. If you can see the devil, then he is outside of you and is no problem. It is when he sneaks in subtly, into your attitudes and thoughts where you can't see him— this is when you need to be afraid of the devil." I felt I had learned a great deal that night.

Internal problems are: 1) unbelief, 2) disobedience, 3) bitterness, and 4) a critical attitude.

If one or several of these internal problems are in your life, external problems will come along and stay problems. They will begin to pound you to pieces and will continue to do so until you get right with God by repentance, obedience, and a sweet spirit towards others.

When the Devil Gets a Foothold

I marvel as I read the book of Judges, chapter 4. The Israelites did evil in the eyes of the Lord. They got an internal problem of disobedience because they were worshipping idols. (Idolatry is, of course, disobedience in one of its strongest forms.) The stage was set for a tragedy.

When an internal problem gets into your life, it is only a matter of time before the devil capitalizes on it and wipes you out with a big external problem.

Such was the case for Israel. Along came a big problem in the form of Jabin, a king of Canaan, who reigned in Hazor. "The commander of his army was Sisera, who lived in Harosheth Haggoyim. Because he had nine hundred iron chariots and had cruelly oppressed the Israelites for twenty years, they cried to the Lord for help," (Judges 4:3, NIV).

Isn't that amazing! It took twenty years of cruel oppression—being pounded to pieces by the curse— before the Israelites were ready to repent! Why did it take them twenty years? Why didn't they repent the first year they were oppressed, or the first month, or the first day?

Again in Judges, Israel sinned. They had another internal problem, and so along came an external problem, Midian. Chapter 6 tells the story of how Midian ravaged the land and totally humiliated and impoverished the Israelites. After seven years of this pounding, they cried out to the Lord for help. Why did it take them seven years? Why didn't they cry out the first year or the first month or the first week or the first day?

Turning at the Lord's Rebuke

I can't answer the question of why the Israelites waited so long. But, I can purpose in my heart that I won't wait that long. Proverbs 1:23 (NAS) says, "Turn to my reproof; behold, I will pour out my Spirit on you. I will make my words known to you".

Years ago I was riding in a car down Interstate 80N along the Columbia River when I read that scripture. My dad was driving, and I was just reading and meditating. I've always wanted God to speak to me, and, I've always wanted his Spirit poured out upon me. So I made a solemn vow to God that was worded something like this: "God, I want to hear your voice and have your Spirit poured out on my life. I want this so badly that I vow to turn at your correction. As often as you look down from heaven and see this long Columbia River, please remember, God, that Wes will turn at your rebuke."

Since that time, I have had some really stiff rebukes, but—I've always turned to God in repentance as quickly as I was aware of my sin or failure.

Don't be afraid of admitting when you are wrong. Quickly admitting failure and getting under the blood of Christ puts you back under the blessing. If you are quick to repent and quick to forgive, you'll experience many miracles in your life.

Proverbs 28:13 (NIV) says, "He who conceals his sin does not prosper, but whoever confesses and renounces them finds mercy." We must be quick to turn at the Lord's rebuke because all of us will make mistakes. But, if we realize that to turn at his rebuke is to turn back under his blessing, why should we wait twenty years, or seven years, or even a single hour? We must begin to value the correction of the Lord that helps us keep on course and under the blessings.

"My son, do not despise the Lord's discipline and do not resent his rebuke, because the Lord disciplines those he loves, as a father the son he delights in," (Proverbs 3:11-12, NIV).

"The corrections of discipline are the way to life," (Proverbs 6:23, NIV).

"It is better to heed a wise man's rebuke than to listen to the song of fools," (Ecclesiastes 7:5, NIV).

Rebukes of wisdom are so precious. They are the way to life. They are the way back under the blood covering provided by Jesus Christ's own sacrifice. That means a rebuke from God is a signpost to point us back toward the blessing from which we have strayed. Value rebukes! Heed them! Turn quickly at his rebuke, and never despise the Lord's discipline.

What is Rebellion?

It is possible for a born again Christian to sin and go to hell, but not accidentally. If a born again Christian sins and goes into rebellion or idolatry, he moves out from under the blood covering. In the book *Angels on Assignment,* Pastor Roland Buck defined rebellion and idolatry as follows:

"To rebel is to refuse allegiance or to resist the authority of someone or some authority over you. God is our authority. To rebel against him is to turn our backs on that which he offers: the protection, the blessings, the love and the promises. Throughout the Bible God plainly spells out the overwhelming blessings which come when we submit to his absolute control, and the curses which come when we resist or rebel against him. Idolatry is excessive attachment or veneration for some person or thing: admiration which borders on adoration. Idolatry is not just worshipping a god or image other than God, it is lusting after our own desires and pleasures, instead of doing what he wants us to do for him," (page 123).

A further definition of rebellion is given in the same book in a preceding chapter: "A shortcoming continued becomes sin, which is rebellion against God, and is not covered by the blood."

This explains the scripture that says, "Not everyone who says to me, 'Lord, Lord,' will enter the kingdom of heaven, but only he who does the will of my Father who is in heaven. Many will say to me on that day, 'Lord, Lord, did we not prophesy in your name, and in your name drive out demons and perform many miracles?' Then I will tell them plainly, 'I never knew you. Away from me, you evildoers!'" (Matthew 7:21-23, NIV).

The people Jesus refers to here were saved at one time. But they became indifferent toward sin, and it became rebellion. They refused to repent and humble themselves under God's correction. They voluntarily moved out from under the blood covering provided by God for their protection.

The Power to Blow It

I used to wonder how God could say that he never "knew" them if they had at one time been used in the gifts of the Spirit and actually preached the gospel. But I understand this now. God is so excited about becoming totally one with us forever that he looked far ahead into the future to see which of us would continue in the shelter of his blood covering. As he looked at the end, he saw those who would continue to abide in him and not move out from under his covering. These he "foreknew." That is, he knew they would make it and began to think about them and the joy that would be eternally his when he finally held them safe in his embrace.

Those whom he knew would voluntarily move out from under his blood covering into rebellion and idolatry he did not foreknow. He saved them when they asked him to, but as he looked at the end and saw the decisions they would make, he did not foreknow them. This doesn't mean he made them grow cold towards him, but it means that he knew they would. Romans 8:29 speaks of those whom God foreknew. God has the ability to know what choices we will make, but he leaves the choices up to us.

Paul was well aware that he had the power to blow it even though he was an apostle. That is why he said, "I beat my body and make it my slave so that, after I have preached to others, I myself will not be disqualified for the prize," (1 Corinthians 9:27 , NIV).

Can you see why we should cherish the corrections of the Lord? What if we were to stray into sin and God did nothing to warn us? When we ended up in hell, we would be most surprised. God loves us so much that if we do get into sin, we can be certain that we'll feel the stroke of divine discipline.

This is evident in the case of King Solomon who drifted from his covenant relationship with God into idolatry—out from under the blood. When a rebuke was not sufficient, God in faithfulness tried to save his soul by sending problems. "Then the Lord raised up against Solomon an adversary, Hadad the Edomite, from the royal line of Edom," (1 Kings 11:14, NIV).

God hoped that this external problem would cause Solomon to see that he was no longer under the blood and under the blessing. This is what the scripture means that says, "Before I was afflicted I went astray, but now I obey your word . . . It was good for me to be afflicted so that I might learn your decrees . . . I know, Oh Lord, that your laws are righteous, and in faithfulness you have afflicted me!" (Psalms 119:67, 71, 75 NIV).

Be careful not to misunderstand this scripture. It is not God's will for you to ever be afflicted by any problem. It is God's will for you to be blessed. But, if you are in rebellion, idolatry, or even ignorant sin (disobedience you are unaware of) then God, in his faithfulness, will allow problems to come your way. When these problems stay problems and do not turn into blessings, check out your life. Make sure you have everything under the blood. God could be warning you, disciplining you to save your soul from being a "castaway".

Coming Into the Light

There is a better way of doing things than being careless until God has to divinely discipline you. "Everyone who does evil hates the light, and will not come into the light for fear that his deeds will be exposed. But whoever lives by the truth comes into the light, so that it may be seen plainly that what he has done has been done through God," (John 3:20-21, NIV).

We need to bring our deeds to God, to the light of his Word, for his examination. We must come to God asking that he would reveal to us anything that is not completely right. As we come to the light, God will always keep us under the blood covering and under the blessings. We'll always be "overcomers" as we change problems into blessings.

We must be like Jesus who said, "The one who sent me is with me; he has not left me alone, for I always do what pleases him," (John 8:29, NIV). There is great safety in having a heart that wants to please God. This is why the Bible says, "Keep your heart with all vigilance and above all that you guard, for out of it flow the springs of life," (Proverbs 4:23, Amplified).

I want to make one other quote from the book *Angels on Assignment:*

"Because we are his, the atoning blood keeps on flowing to cleanse us all the time. We are not cleansed just by verbal confession, because our lips can say words we don't mean. Our true confession comes from the heart when our sincere desire is to please him. God loves us so much he wants us to know that we don't have to be on pins and needles in his presence, plagued by fear of failure in word, thought, or deed. When little things divert our attention, a little temper rises or a bad attitude creeps in, and we forget to ask God's forgiveness for it, he looks at our hearts and our intentions. We are justified under the new law because of what Jesus did when he died for us, and that precious blood continues to cleanse as long as we want to stay under the covering God provided, and he has also provided guiding signals from his Holy Spirit which are ever present to keep us under his covering," (page 118).

Certainly, we should want always to please him and come to the light to see if what we are doing is pleasing him. Then we will not come under the chastening rod. Just a word of rebuke will be enough for us.

"A rod is for the back of him who lacks judgment," (Proverbs 26:3, NIV).

"A whip for the horse, a halter for the donkey, and a rod for the back of fools," (Proverbs 26:3, NIV).

"Rebuke a wise man, and he will be wiser still; teach a righteous man and he will add to his learning," (Proverbs 9:8b-9, NIV).

Do you see, then, that God's method of correction is his Word, and that problems and difficulties sent by God are strictly last-ditch efforts to save a Christian from physical judgement or even eternal death?

"My brothers, if one of you should wander from the truth and someone should bring him back, remember this: whoever turns a sinner away from his error will save him from death and cover over a multitude of sins," (James 5:19-20, NIV). This verse is further proof that a brother can wander from the truth and be called a sinner headed for spiritual death.

The Shipwreck of Faith

The Bible says, "I give you this instruction . . . so that by following them you may fight the good fight, holding on to faith and a good conscience. Some have rejected these and so have shipwrecked their faith," (l Timothy 1:18-19, NIV). I would like to give you an illustration as to how a person shipwrecks his faith.

NO EXTERNAL PROBLEM CAN SINK YOUR SHIP!!

EXTERNAL PROBLEM

EXTERNAL PROBLEM

CHRISTIAN WITH A RIGHT SPIRIT

"AND WE KNOW THAT GOD CAUSES ALL THINGS TO WORK TOGETHER FOR GOOD FOR THOSE WHO LOVE GOD, TO THOSE WHO ARE THE CALLED ACCORDING TO HIS PURPOSE." ROM. 8:28-NAS

Suppose you are the captain of a giant battleship. Your ship is armed with the most expensive weaponry money can buy. Radar tracks all incoming enemy planes, and before they can unleash their lethal dose of destruction, your guns shoot each one of them down.

This is the way it is as a Christian. But "the weapons we fight with are not the weapons of the world. On the contrary, they have divine power to demolish strongholds," (2 Corinthians 10: 4, NIV). Our spiritual weapons have the ability to shoot down every external problem and to "overcome" each one.

In the most fierce persecution, there is no need to be overcome by the problem. Even death as a martyr would

91

turn into a blessing because you would receive a martyr's crown and great heavenly treasure for suffering for Christ!

You are the captain of your life. You hold the wheel which turns the rudder. In other words, you have a free will and can turn any way you want. God is like Command Headquarters. He gives instructions and briefings and battle plans and provides the equipment, but the rudder is in your hands. You steer your life. If you shipwreck, it will be because of your wrong steering, not God's.

Headed For Disaster

In our illustration, suppose that in the course of shooting down the enemy airplane, the ship strays off course in the heat of the battle. Command Headquarters speaks to the captain and tells him to readjust his course—that he has strayed into dangerous waters. Command Headquarters repeats the instructions many times, but the captain refuses to turn the wheel. He refuses to believe that he got off course.

ONLY AN *INTERNAL* PROBLEM CAN SINK YOUR SHIP.

INTERNAL PROBLEM: A SPIRIT THAT WON'T REPENT OF GUILT—A WRONG SPIRIT.

I DID NOT MAKE A WRONG TURN. AS FAR AS I'M CONCERNED I'M RIGHT ON COURSE.

"IF YOU HAD RESPONDED TO MY REBUKE, I WOULD HAVE POURED OUT MY HEART TO YOU..." PROV. 1:23 N.I.V.

This can happen in a Christian's life. When God's Spirit convicts us and says we are off course, or if the Word of God plainly shows us that we are, then we are foolish if we are too embarrassed to admit it. If we refuse to correct our course and get back where we should be, we have an internal problem.

Let's look at our battleship again. Now the captain has made up his mind that if there was an error, it has been on the part of the Command Headquarters. He strays into waters that have icebergs in them, and a heavy fog sets in. Vision becomes impaired in the fog. Even though the radar screen indicates large icebergs ahead, the captain thinks there must be something wrong with the radar. Soon the ship has strayed too far and tears itself open on a giant iceberg and sinks rapidly.

"BUT SINCE YOU IGNORED ALL MY ADVICE...I WILL MOCK...WHEN CALAMITY OVERTAKES YOU LIKE A STORM..." PROV. 1:24-27

This is what can happen to a Christian. When an internal problem develops, the devil will be quick to exploit this situation with the biggest external problems possible. The stage is set for spiritual shipwreck. Inside the Christian, the conscience is going wild with warnings. But the "radar" is ignored, or else it is assumed that the voice of the conscience is the voice of self or the devil, not really the voice of God speaking through our human spirit. Into these dangerous waters the wandering Christian strays.

When the big tragedy occurs, the iceberg—the problem—is blamed for causing the wreck. The final step of this ignorance is to blame it on God. "Why did God put the iceberg in my way? God did it! It is God's fault!"

As the ship sinks, the captain drowns and blames God all the way down. But it wasn't God's fault. He had warned about the com-

THE SHIPWRECK OF FAITH.

THE FINAL DISASTER IS SPIRITUAL DEATH. BY REFUSING TO REPENT OF WRONGDOING THE PERSON BLAMES GOD—ALL THE WAY DOWN.

EXTERNAL PROBLEM

IT'S GOD'S FAULT! IT ABSOLUTELY WASN'T MY FAULT! WHY DID GOD PUT THAT ICEBERG IN MY WAY?

"YOU MAY BE SURE THAT YOUR SIN WILL FIND YOU OUT." NUMBERS 32:23 N.I.V.

ing disaster. He warned about the internal problem. It wasn't really the iceberg that sunk the ship—it was an internal problem in the captain, for he could have sailed the ship away from the dangerous waters.

Christians, this is a sobering thought. It is possible for you to shipwreck your faith if you don't listen to God and obey him. We also may be responsible for the spiritual death of others if we are in a position of authority. If a Christian husband shipwrecks his faith, it may throw his entire family into such chaos that his children or wife would also shipwreck their faith.

The higher our position of authority, the more careful we must be lest others follow us in error. This is why the Bible says, "Not many of you should presume to be teachers, my brothers, because you know that we who teach will be judged more strictly," (James 3:1, NIV).

Those in government must also be especially careful. We must remember that when King Jeroboam made shipwreck of his faith and went into idolatry, the ten nation tribes of Israel followed him into sin. They never came out of idolatry, and the whole nation was later destroyed.

When a marriage, a ministry, or a government sinks because of the sins of the leader, all who are involved with him are endangered greatly. If, however, these other people retain a "right spirit," God will preserve them, and they will survive the shipwreck experience. Even the person whose

error has caused a shipwreck can survive if, before death, he takes the blame and repents. Remember Jonah, who was nearly dead but just at the last moment called out to God in repentance.

Deeper Lessons

Earlier in this book I wrote part of a song God gave to me called "Basic Intercession." I want to repeat it:

"When you learn the lesson
'Basic Intercession',
deeper lessons will come to your heart.
But till you intercede
for your brother's small need,
real travail you're not ready to start."

When we learn "basic intercession," we learn to overlook faults, stop gossip, cast down vain imaginations, promote love, keep unity, cover character faults with our love, etc. Few Christians are even good at this simple form of intercession. This simple form will do a great deal for any church or individual and prevent church splits and squabbles over small things.

However, there is a need for the deeper lessons of travail. Basic intercession does not deal with interceding for those who are lost and hellbound because of persistent and unconfessed sins, whether these people are heathen or wandering Christians. Basic intercession just helps us to love each other better and not to dwell on each other's shortcomings, the little faults men see in imperfect Christians but which are covered by the blood.

Travail in the Spirit for one who is lost because of sin is surely a "deeper lesson" that God wants to teach us. Thousands of unsaved people will go to hell if intercessors who know how to travail in prayer do not arise. Also, many Christians who have greatly erred from the faith will be lost if intercessors do not arise and do something about their need.

You will remember that the Galatians were born again, but the entire church got into false doctrine. They were all in danger of losing their salvation, but Paul rose up in the Spirit and did something about them. He writes, "My little children, of whom I travail in birth again until Christ be formed in you. . ." (Galatians 4:19, KJV). When they were lost and without God, Paul travailed in the Spirit until they were saved. When they were losing out with God because of slipping into false doctrine, Paul said he travailed again.

Isaiah 53:11 (KJV) says this about Jesus, "He shall see the travail of his soul and be satisfied".

I want to be satisfied. I'm not satisfied if I only see mediocre results from my soul-winning efforts. I want real satisfaction at seeing thousands upon thousands come to Christ as a result of my life. To have that kind of satisfaction, as Jesus had, I know I must also have travail of soul—that great spirit of prayer that brings down revival.

I think of the scripture that says, "For as soon as Zion travailed she brought forth her children," (Isaiah 66:7, KJV).

This verse may refer to Israel becoming a nation in one day after World War II. But it also has a spiritual message for us. If we will travail, we'll bring forth spiritual children.

Paul also writes in Romans 8:26-27 (NIV), "In the same way, the Spirit helps us in our weakness. We do not know what we ought to pray, but the Spirit himself intercedes for us with groans that words cannot express. And he who searches our hearts knows the mind of the Spirit because the Spirit intercedes for the saints in accordance with God's will."

Certainly, we can appropriate this wonderful promise by praying in the Spirit (in tongues unknown to us). Let us dedicate ourselves to obeying Paul's command to "be faithful in prayer," (Romans 12:12, NIV). Let us master the basics of intercession and move on into the deeper lessons of travail, remembering that in prayer we are generating power to help us reach our goal: the salvation of souls!

10
DISCERNMENT VERSUS PRIDE

The Bible says in Psalms 36:1-4 (NIV), "An oracle is within my heart concerning the sinfulness of the wicked. There is no fear of God before his eyes. For in his own eyes he flatters himself too much to detect or hate his sin. The words of his mouth are wicked and deceitful; he has ceased to be wise and to do good. Even on his bed he plots evil; he commits himself to a sinful course and does not reject what is wrong."

This verse explains the scripture that says, "Pride goes before destruction, a haughty spirit before a fall," (Proverbs 16:18, NIV). Why do many who are used of God fall? Because they lose their ability to detect or hate sin. They lose this sense of discernment—the ability to tell the difference between right ways and wrong ways when they begin to receive the praise of men.

First comes flattery, or the praise of men. Maybe the person praises himself, or perhaps many others are praising him. When he starts to believe the praise or flattery of men and receives it rather than turning it to God, his discernment leaves.

Without discernment, it is only a matter of time before this person falls into some serious error. As the Scripture has said, "He flatters himself too much to detect or hate his sin . . . he has ceased to be wise and to do good."

This means that once he was wise, and once he did good. We must learn how to give glory to God and live for his praise alone and not receive the praise of men. Then we will always keep our ability to discern right from wrong, and we will not fall. We will be able to handle success and not let it go to our heads and puff us up. God wants to raise up men and women of God who can handle the success he wants them to have! Our prayer should be, "God, help me be a master at giving you the glory!"

Why We Need Discernment

Discernment is a wonderful thing that will keep us from falling. With it, we can detect sin. When we goof, we can see it or feel it. Our conscience works. We must be very careful to remember that with Christ we can do all things but without him we are nothing.

Our discernment will leave us when pride comes. The Bible says about Samson, "He awoke from his sleep and thought, 'I'll go out as before and shake myself free.' But he did not know that the Lord had left him," (Judges 16:20, NIV).

Many mighty men of God who were used to do miracles by the power of the Spirit have suddenly awakened to find that the pride and flattery they had cuddled up to (like Delilah) had cut off their discernment (like Samson's hair), and they were powerless before the onslaught of the enemy who had been longing for the day and hour he could ruin and destroy them. The praise of men may look like a beautiful thing to receive, but if you cuddle up to it and listen to its smooth words of flattery, you are in big trouble.

"WHOEVER FLATTERS HIS NEIGHBOR IS SPREADING A NET FOR HIS FEET." PROV. 29:5

"Whoever flatters his neighbor is spreading a net for his feet," (Proverbs 29:5, NIV).

"When pride comes, then comes disgrace, but with humility comes wisdom," (Proverbs 11:2, NIV).

If you value wisdom and discernment and you believe that these are wonderful qualities to possess, then you must realize that you must go without the praise of men in order to have them. The old saying, "You can't have your cake and eat it, too" means that you can't have the pretty cake to look at and still have the joy of eating it. You have to make the choice of keeping it to look at or eating it.

If you want to be greatly used of God, you must make a quality decision to live for the praise that comes from God, and reject the praise and flattery that come from men. You cannot have both. If you choose to start receiving praise and flattery from men, you have just chosen to reject wisdom and discernment.

Glorifying the Father

Jesus is our pattern. He lived his earthly life as a man to show us how to live as men. He said, "I do not accept praise from men, (John 5:41, NIV). He came in his Father's name.

"When he came near the place where the road goes down the Mount of Olives, the whole crowd of disciples began joyfully to praise God in loud voices for all the miracles they had seen: 'Blessed is the king who comes   in the name of the Lord!'" (Luke 19:37-38). His Father was getting the praise, and the Pharisees knew it. But they were angry because the people were confessing that Jesus was the king–the Messiah! Jesus always turned the praise of the crowd to God. He did not receive it himself but gave it to God. His glory was to glorify his Father. This should be our glory, the glory of glorifying the Father.

When Christ rebuked the Pharisees in Matthew 23, he said, "Everything they do is done for men to see," (verse 5,

NIV). Because Christ doesn't want his followers to fall into sin, he has instructed us to do many things in secret so that no man would be able to praise us. Then, we live for the secret praise of God that is communicated to our spirits, "You are doing good! I'm so pleased with you. Keep it up. You are doing what I want done."

We must actually take great delight in doing things that no one but God will ever know about. We know we cannot receive the praise of men if men do not even know what we have done.

It is not possible to do everything for God in secret. However, there are some things that we can do in secret such as giving money, praying, and fasting. In Matthew 6:1-18 Jesus gives instructions about these three secret areas and how we can show our love for God. He promises, "Your Father, who sees what is done in secret, will reward you," (verse 18, NIV).

The night before I was to preach a revival service, I was awakened by the Holy Spirit at about 3:00 a.m. I got up and went over to the church, which was next door to my home, to keep from awakening my wife. I had planned on preaching another sermon, but the Lord wanted me to preach on the Word of God and how wonderful it is.

As I began to worship the Lord and praise him for his Word, I was saying something like this: "Oh, Father, I love your Word. I worship you for your Word. I want you to know that I give my whole life over to you to fill with your Word. I want to belong totally to the Word of God and have it become flesh in me and live in me."

As I was telling God things along this line, suddenly the Spirit spoke to me and said something like this: "All right, I'll accept you at your word. You will be totally mine. You shall belong to the Word, and the Word will be your entire life. But, I'll be jealous over you—extremely jealous, since you are giving yourself totally to me. This means you will have great success. If at the height of that success, you prostitute yourself by accepting the praise of men, you will be committing adultery against me. If you turn from your deep love for me and embrace their praises instead of living for mine alone, I will then reveal to the world that you are an adulterer. I will withdraw from you, and you will fall into sins of the flesh. They may not be able to tell when you are committing spiritual adultery by accepting their praises, so if you break my heart by turning from me to embrace their flatteries, I will withdraw from you until you commit sins that they can see, and then everyone will know what you are."

The day before God spoke to me about this, I had been talking to another preacher about a well-known evangelist. This man had filled great auditoriums, and many miracles had happened under his ministry. At the height of all this, he was found having sex with a young boy. I couldn't understand how a man who knew God in such a powerful way could goof up so badly. But when God spoke those things to my heart early in the morning in that church office, I knew why.

I purposed deep within my heart to live for God's praise alone and to flee from people who would lavish flattery upon me.

Encouragement or Flattery?

What God told me was so heavy that I trembled. I sat there quietly and thought for a long time about his message to me. I prayed for the man who had fallen and asked God to totally restore him and deliver him from the subtle enemy of pride that had taken away his sense of discernment to the point that he could no longer detect or hate sin.

Then, I saw how important it was for laymen to realize these things. They must learn not to flatter the men of God whom they love and admire. Everyone needs to be encouraged and appreciated. But, we need to draw a line between appreciation and praise of men—between encouragement and flattery. God, who gives wisdom liberally to all who ask in faith, will help us to do this.

When I was growing up on my dad's cattle ranch in South Dakota, I would work really hard so that my dad would tell me that I had done a good job. When we would finish a big job and come into the house, he would have a smile on his face that told me he felt a great sense of accomplishment. Then he would laugh and say, "We did good, boy. We hoed out our row."

I suppose the expression "Hoe out your row" is not understood much anymore. But in the old days when people worked in their gardens, they had to hoe the weeds out with an old fashioned hoe. It was not a good idea to quit in the middle of a row, so they would always at least finish the row they were hoeing before quitting time. This was one of my dad's favorite sayings, and it has become one of mine as well.

I loved to receive a word of praise from my father and would go to great extremes to get it. I knew that if I were out mowing a hay field, I could get a special word of thanks and appreciation if I finished the field up before coming in for supper. So, I'd often stay out late and get a cold supper if I had to so that I could come in and grin and say, "I hoed out my row." This sense of accomplishment, and my dad saying, "You did good, boy, you hoed out your row," made all the extra work seem more than worth it.

Now, I'm saying this to show you the difference between telling someone that they have done good, and flattering them. I believe in telling people when they have done good. There is a way to do this so that they want to keep it up and do more.

When I was a bus director, I would always stay at the church until the last bus driver returned because I wanted to thank each one of them and tell them they did good.

This kept a lot of them going, and I expressed my love for them by telling them how much I appreciated their help. There's nothing wrong with that.

It's hard for me to communicate with mere words the difference between puffing someone up and building someone up. We need to build one another up. Perhaps it could be explained by the words of Jesus when he said, "Give to Caesar what is Caesar's and to God what is God's," (Mark 12:17, NIV).

When we give men thanks and appreciation that belongs to them because of loyal and hard work, we do rightly. But when we give to men glory that belongs to God, we do wrongly. We must be careful not to want the glory and praise that belongs to God, for there are always men who are more than willing to give to men the glory that belongs to God alone.

<u>Giving God All the Glory</u>

I was able to see Kathryn Kuhlman in person only once when she was holding a service in Portland, Oregon. There were many miracles, and she preached a good message. But what fascinated me was one phrase she said over and over during the miracle service: "We vow to give you all the glory." There was a tone and force to her voice when she said "vow" that I could never forget. It was intense and zealous and determined, and it has echoed in my spirit ever since. "We vow to give you all the glory."

Whenever I see someone who is greatly used of God, I want to know if he is doing something that I could also do so that I might be used of God in a greater way. So I look for clues that would reveal the reason for his success. It was obvious with Kathryn Kuhlman. She gave God all the glory for the miracles that were being done.

Many times I have wanted to say what she said, "I vow to give you the glory, Lord." But, I used to wonder, "Am I really giving him all the glory? How can I really know that in my heart I 'm not hanging on to some little part of it?" It seems to me that it takes a good deal of wisdom to be able to give God the glory, since pride can be very subtle and sneak in easily. So my prayer has been, "God, give me the wisdom to give you the glory, and I promise I'll do it."

It is my desire that when I vow to give him all the glory, I will know that I am, indeed, keeping the vow. I pray almost daily, "God, help me to be a master at giving you glory."

May God deliver us from desiring to draw men's attention to our person, and may God grant that we can draw men's attention to Christ. May God grant to us humility and discernment and wisdom and love so that our light will shine before men in such a way that they will see our good works but will glorify our Father in Heaven.

When I moved to Omaha, Nebraska, to pioneer a new church, I had to look for weeks to find a building where we could meet. During these weeks, I worshiped in various churches in the community. One Sunday, I was especially moved during the song service of a church I was visiting. I was crying and telling the Lord I wanted to do great things for him, but that I wanted him to get all the glory. Suddenly, God spoke to me.

"WHEN YOU WIN THE CROWN, DON'T BOW DOWN AND WORSHIP YOUR IMAGE IN IT," he said.

In my mind, I could see a man holding a shiny, gold crown, looking at his own reflection in the crown. Instead of casting the crown at the feet of the Lord, he was bowing down and worshipping his own reflection in his crowning achievement!

Immediately I knew that this has happened over and over in the body of Christ. Ministers depend on God and are greatly used because of this dependency. When the great achievement comes, many fail to give the glory to

God and take the credit themselves. In effect, they move into idolatry while at the height of their ministry. They began to worship themselves. Their ministries corrupt, and they fall.

Pride Busters

For years, besides "sweet spirit verses, I've been collecting other verses I call PRIDE BUSTERS. Here is the ultimate "pride buster": "The overseer . . . must not be a recent convert, or he may become conceited and fall under the same judgment as the devil," (I Tim. 3:1, 6, NIV).

Pride, or conceit, is idolatry, the worship of self. If any pastor or Christian wins a crown (achieves something significant with God's help), he must cast this at the Lord's feet and worship the Lord, not himself.

If he does not cast it at the Lord's feet, but rather bows down to worship his achievement (really himself), he becomes an idolater and will share the same judgment as the devil. That means he'd go to hell if he died. We must tremble at the thought. God will NOT share his glory with another.

"I am the Lord, that is my name! I will not give my glory to another or my praise to idols," (Isaiah 42:8, NIV).

Remember brethren, ONLY THE HUMBLE will inherit the kingdom of God. Past deeds of righteousness will not be rewarded if you make your achievements an idol. No wonder Christ said, "Not everyone who says to me, 'Lord, Lord', will enter the kingdom of heaven, but only he who does the will of my Father who is in heaven. Many will say to me on that day, 'Lord, Lord, did we not prophesy in your name, and in your name drive out demons and perform many miracles?' Then I will tell them plainly, 'I never knew you. Away from me, you evildoers!'" (Matt. 7:21-23 NIV).

One day I preached our 8:00 a.m. service and took a prayer walk while I waited for the next service at 10:45 a.m.

A voice spoke to my mind and said, "You sure are a great preacher, Wes. You preach so well. That was absolutely fabulous!" Immediately, I knew the devil was trying to get me to touch the glory of God.

God helped me to respond like this:

"Satan, I know that is you. The sermon <u>was</u> wonderful because it was God's truth. It <u>was</u> wonderful because of God's anointing."

The voice responded, "Yes, but your voice inflection–the way <u>you</u> put it across, others can't do it that well."

"Satan," I said, "The Bible says 'Do not worry about what to say or how to say it. At that time you will be given what to say, for it will not be you speaking, but the Spirit of your Father speaking through you,'" (Matt. 10:19-20 NIV).

Then I continued, "I'm <u>NOT</u> a great preacher, but the HOLY SPIRIT IS! He gave me what to say and how to say it!"

Then I said, "Father, I give you all the glory! You helped me and your truth and anointing made it wonderful. Be so gracious as to do it again at 10:45." Then the presence of the Lord enveloped me, and the flattering thoughts ceased. Satan had fled.

Beloved, the minute you pray for someone and they get healed, or you have a prophecy or word of knowledge, or you cast out a demon, be sure that the devil will be there to congratulate you. He wants you on his side, so if you won't be on his side by selling drugs or being a prostitute, he'll be happy to have you be a glory robber, a religious idolater, a spiritual adulterer. So be on your guard to resist him. Because you can resist him, and when you do, he will flee!

Keep casting your crowns at the Lord's feet, and you'll walk in the Lord's discernment and spend eternity in God's presence. Pray earnestly for the Holy Spirit to help you know all the different ways of giving glory to God. May you and I always be found faithful in this matter.

One day I was out walking and talking with the Lord. I asked, "Father, what is the key word in being a great achiever?"

The Lord said, "DEPENDENCY." That was not what I had imagined he'd say. I thought it would be diligence or persistence.

Then the Lord gave me a great sermon called THE CYCLE OF SUCCESS. The entire message is a "pride buster". Here it is briefly.

The Cycle of Success

There are seven steps in The Cycle of Success. They are:

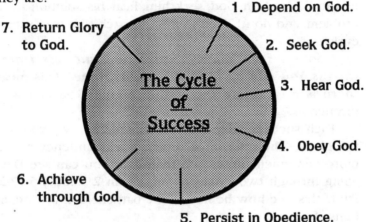

1. **Depend on God.**

7. **Return Glory to God.**

2. **Seek God.**

The Cycle of Success

3. **Hear God.**

4. **Obey God.**

6. **Achieve through God.**

5. **Persist in Obedience.**

God showed me, "*No man is a success. Only God is a success.*" We can "cycle in success" with God, but the minute we depend on ourselves, thinking how great we are, we've broken the cycle.

Every king in the Bible broke the cycle. In fact, very few Bible heroes had an unbroken series of success cycles.

God explained to me that the sixth step was his step. All achievement that counts for anything is what God has done through us. That's why he must get all the praise.

Psalms 127:1 (NIV) says "Unless the Lord builds the house, its builders labor in vain. Unless the Lord watches over the city, the watchmen stand guard in vain." (That's a pride buster of a scripture!)

I'm doing my best to avoid a blowout of this cycle. So far, I've not had a blowout of disobedience or a failure to depend on or seek God or to give him the glory. But I have had some slow leaks.

A slow leak is when you fail to depend on God in some smaller decision. In my case, I hired some staff members I shouldn't have. I <u>thought</u> I had heard from God, but in fact, I moved in haste. I paid dearly for this mistake. Success in my ministry kept leaking out. In order to plug the leak, I had to depend on God, seek him, hear his solution to the problem, and do it! Then things got back to a true success cycle.

God told me, *"You will never be a succcess. I am a success. You can cycle in success with me."* This means there is no limit to the achievements God can work through us.

Each success cycle must be completed by giving God the glory. Then we must return to dependency and be more dependent upon him than ever. You can see David going through two cycles of success in 2 Samuel 5:17-22. Study this. See how he named the battlefield after God, not himself.

One last word about pride. If you are a pastor, pay special attention. When the proud get into positions of authority in the church, being a pastor becomes miserable. If we can somehow keep the proud out of every authorative position, the ministry is smooth sailing and a real joy. There is no form of church government that can work effectively if the prideful are in control. However, if the humble are in authority, even more cumbersome forms of church government can function well.

Early in my pastorate, I took new people and gave them positions of responsibility far too quickly. They appeared talented and gifted, so I quickly made them home fellowship group leaders, adult Sunday School teachers, even staff members. And I got burned!

I learned to watch people several months to determine their true immunity level. If they gave strong evidence of being truly humble, I opened the door to major responsibility.

New people can be involved immediately in the work of God, but not in leadership positions. Prove the new people first in jobs where they are under authority. If they do well, in God's time you can give them authority. You'll save yourself untold heartaches if you are careful in this area.

11
THE TEST OF TEARS

The more knowledge I acquire and the more under-standing I get, the more love I need to stay balanced. Remember that the Bible says, "If I can fathom all mysteries and all knowledge . . . but have not love, I am nothing," (1 Corinthians 13:2, NIV).

You must have gained some knowledge and insight from reading this book. But now you need to make sure you gain love. Why? Because if your knowledge of right and wrong increases, but your love does not, you will be out of balance.

You can test yourself to determine if you are being judgmental when you see someone's sins. It is the test of tears.

Love is the great balancer. If you think anyone's life is out of balance, and you want to correct this by your prayers, you can start by praying that their love will abound more and more. A person can get out of balance if he speaks in tongues but doesn't have love. Love will balance that out. If a person has the gift of prophecy, he can get out of balance if he doesn't have enough love. If a person can fathom all mysteries and all knowledge, he really needs love to be balanced. If a person has faith that can move mountains, he will need love or else he'll be out of balance. If a person is a great giver, he'll need to do it from love to stay balanced. Love will balance everyone. (See 1 Corinthians 13:1-3.)

There is a responsibility that comes with spiritual gifts. That responsibility is to get love so that these gifts of God will not be misused. Paul said, "The only thing that counts is faith expressing itself through love," (Galatians 5:6, NIV).

Many people are getting lots of faith but are not getting an equivalent amount of love. As a result, they judge other people if they are sick. They use their faith for themselves but rarely use it to win souls. They need more love.

This is why you need to be careful about just listening to one man of God. If that man of God mainly preaches about faith, you must get some teaching about love somewhere or you'll get out of balance.

It is the same with knowledge. You could turn into a real miserable person if you get a lot of faith or a lot of knowledge, but don't have much love. You might be satisfied with yourself, but you'll be miserable to be around because you'll always be judging other people. You'll set yourself up as a judge, and your little gavel of condemnation towards others less spiritual than you will be banging the desk often as you pronounce them "guilty."

God wants you to be like a defense attorney, not a judge or a prosecutor. God is the judge. Satan is an accuser. God wants us to be like Jesus, an advocate who ever lives to make intercession for us.

Some people will read this book and their knowledge will be increased. But they will not earnestly pray for love. As a result, they will not become the kind of person God wants them to be. Knowledge and wisdom and understanding and discernment are wonderful qualities if they have love to go along and balance them.

Need More Love?

How can you tell if you need more love? When love sees someone fall into sin, it cries. Tears come.

Take Jonah and Jeremiah, for example. Both had the gift of prophecy, but Jonah was out of balance because he had little love. He sat on a hill overlooking Nineveh and waited for God to fulfill his prophetic words of judgment. There was not a tear in his eye. His anger burned toward the city and he eagerly anticipated the fiery judgment of God.

How disappointed he was when God forgave the people and did not destroy them. Jonah failed the test of tears.

Jeremiah, however, was known as the weeping prophet. He had a bitter message of judgment and destruction for a stubborn and wicked people. But, it broke his heart to see their shameful end as famine and war came upon them. "Oh, that my head were a spring of water and my eyes a fountain of tears! I would weep day and night for the slain of my people," (Jeremiah 9:1, NIV).

"But if you do not listen, I will weep in secret because of your pride; my eyes will weep bitterly, overflowing with tears, because the Lord's flock will be taken captive," (Jeremiah 13:17, NIV).

"Let my eyes overflow with tears night and day without ceasing; for my virgin daughter—my people—has suffered a grievous wound, a crushing blow," (Jeremiah 14:17, NIV).

"My eyes fail from weeping, I am in torment within, my heart is poured out on the ground because my people are destroyed, because children and infants faint in the streets of the city," (Lamentations 2:11, NIV).

It is easy to see that Jeremiah had a loving heart that did not wish evil to come upon anyone.

I have had God reveal things to me about people— how they had sinned and what was going to come upon them as a result. What do you do when God tells you that a person has sinned and that judgment will come? If you don't have love, you just wait and watch for it to happen as Jonah did. But if you have love, you'll go to prayer and your compassion will reveal itself through your tears. If you have no tears, you need more love. If you can see that a person is in serious trouble, but you don't care, and you don't cry, you need more love.

So what if you can tell that a man's ministry will be ruined or that his teaching is getting into error? So what if you know what his end result will be? What counts is real compassion to accompany this knowledge, and most people come up severely short of tears.

"With Many Tears"

Paul, who was one of the greatest intercessors ever, said, "I served the Lord with great humility and with tears, although I was severely tested by the plots of the Jews . . . Remember that for three years I never stopped warning each of you night and day with tears," (Acts 20:19,31, NIV). He said this to the Ephesians, and he also wrote to the Corinthians, "For I wrote you out of great distress and anguish of heart and with many tears, not to grieve you but to let you know the depth of my love for you," (2 Corinthians 2:4, NIV).

The letter he speaks of was 1 Corinthians, which deals with more problems than does any other epistle. A lesser man would have written a strong letter like 1 Corinthians in a spirit of anger and judgment. Paul wrote it with tears.

I hope each of you will take the test of tears often. Before you talk about a brother who is doing something wrong, ask yourself, "Have I wept for him?" Before you gossip about some sister's shortcomings, have you prayed for her with tears? Knowledge will be of little help if we aren't compassionate.

Another example of Paul's loving intercession is found in Philippians 3:18-19, NIV: "For as I have often told you before and now say again even with tears, many live as enemies of the cross of Christ. Their destiny is destruction, their god is their stomach, and their glory is in their shame. Their mind is on earthly things." Paul said some very strong words about the "enemies of the cross," but he said it with tears, sorrowing for their fate and praying for them.

It is easy to judge and condemn people who are in error. Real spirituality will express itself in tears when souls are erring into destruction. If we do not have enough compassion to weep for the people we criticize, perhaps it would be better not to criticize them at all.

It is necessary to warn congregations of any false teaching, but in our warnings let us not forget to pray for those who are spreading the false doctrine. When our warnings about these people have to be strongly worded, we should take the test of tears before we speak out against them. Let us warn others about error—and weep for those who err. In this way, we will save others by keeping them from believing false doctrine and safeguard ourselves by keeping a pure attitude.

Paul wrote, "Who is weak, and I do not feel weak? Who is led into sin, and I do not inwardly burn?" (2 Corinthians 11:29). May God help us to burn with compassion and with hot tears instead of burning with anger and judgment. May God deliver us from being apathetic about a brother or sister who falls into sin. Let us pray for this kind of compassion that goes beyond just basic intercession and moves into real travail in the Spirit. May God help you to be that kind of a man or woman of prayer.

12
SO THAT NOTHING WILL HINDER YOUR PRAYERS

The Bible says, "Husbands, in the same way, be <u>considerate</u> as you live with your wives, and treat them with <u>respect</u> as the weaker partner and as heirs with you of the gracious gift of life so that nothing will hinder your prayers," (I Peter 3:7, NIV).

It is a fact that bad attitudes in the home hinder prayers. However, if we <u>do</u> show consideration and respect the opposite is true—our prayers are enhanced, because "faith worketh by love" (Gal. 5:6, KJV). According to God—love in the home is a true <u>FOUNDATION</u> of effective prayer.

My wife, Bonnie, is a beautiful lady, and we've been in love since January of 1971 when we began dating. We've never been unfaithful to each other, neither of us ever smoked, drank alcoholic beverages, or experimented with street drugs. We've always tithed and attended church. But I unknowingly laid a stumbling block in our marriage with my over-commitment to the ministry.

I began in the ministry soon after we were married, and for the next several years I worked an average of 84 hours a week doing church work. My marriage was deteriorating due to neglect, but I was not aware of it.

Then I resigned as associate pastor and began to travel as an evangelist. Bonnie and our new daughter, Heather, accompanied me on most trips. We did this for eighteen months before moving to Omaha to pioneer Living Faith Church.

This move devastated my wife who had to leave her parents, her brothers, her house, horse, mountains and the ocean she loved. She had lost her husband years ago to a mistress named "ministry" and now this "ministry" was taking away nearly everything else she held dear. She was convinced that I did not love her. If I got her to admit that it was <u>God</u> who led me to Omaha, not myself, then she felt <u>God</u> didn't love her.

When my wife was nervous and hostile, I defended myself in a way that only made things worse. Before long we both reached the point of wishing we could die to escape. (We did not consider divorce to be an option.)

Once while on vacation in Florida, we were in so much strife we could not agree on how to cross a parking lot. I was sure the problem was with my wife—if she'd only shape up! But God would never side with me against her. He'd only tell me how to love her.

For years I begged God to let me move back to Oregon. "Please don't make me your kidnapper," I pleaded. "I'll do anything for you myself, but please don't make me force my wife to stay here when she wants to be somewhere else." God only reminded me of Moses who had nearly one million people feeling like he had kidnapped them! God refused to let me go back to Oregon.

Then for two years I looked for acreage outside of Omaha. I felt if I got my wife a big enough house in the country, with a nice horse barn, it would solve my problem and she'd be happy in Nebraska. Nothing opened up. God closed that door and failed my expectations. But he did not fail!

All along his plan was to take away Bonnie's comfort zone so that *he* could become her comfort zone. He was not interested in having me create a new one. Equal to that in importance, God wanted to teach me how to give myself to my wife. It was only when all other possibilities of making my wife happy were exhausted that God got my full attention. Then he taught me how to love my wife as

Christ loved the church. God changed our marriage by changing me and turned our pain into a stream of healing for other marriages. Now I'll show you the three key areas of truth that can heal your marriage and strengthen your prayer life.

#1 Reorganize Your Priorities

God began to change me with a lesson about priorities. I was reading the story of Jephthah in Judges, chapter eleven.

Jephthah told God that if God would give him victory in battle, he'd sacrifice as a burnt offering the first person that came out of his house to meet him upon his return. When he returned triumphantly his only daughter ran out to joyfully greet him. He sadly kept his vow and soon her beautiful young body was nothing but ashes in the wind.

"God," I protested, "that is the sickest story in the Bible. Why did you even put it in there?"

"I put it in there for people like you," God answered. Then God explained I was a Jephthah—thinking God desired the sacrifice of my family in order to achieve victory in the ministry.

GOD <u>DOESN'T</u> DESIRE THE FAMILY TO BE SACRIFICED! And he let me know he was not pleased with my misguided devotion that resulted in 84-hour work weeks and hardly any family time.

"Where priorities are wrong, relationships are strained," God taught me. Then he showed me what I call the "Pyramid of Priorities."

From the bottom, building up to the

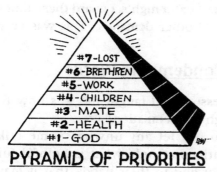

PYRAMID OF PRIORITIES

#7-LOST
#6-BRETHREN
#5-WORK
#4-CHILDREN
#3-MATE
#2-HEALTH
#1-GOD

peak, we start with God. Our relationship with him must be our number one priority.

Number two is our health because as God taught me, "A dead servant can't serve anybody."

Number three should be our mate; number four, our children; number five, our work; number six, our brethren; and number seven, the pinnacle or "focus" of all priorities should be the "lost."

Before this lesson, I felt guilty taking time off with the family just to enjoy them.

When I forced myself to take a day off, my wife would ask, "Are you taking this day off just for me?"

I'd say, "Yes, of course, I'm taking it off for you."

She'd respond angrily, "Then just go work at the church!"

"What does that woman want," I'd complain. "She wants me to take time off with her, and when I do she throws a fit!"

What she wanted was to be assured I was taking time off not because she had begged me to, but because I WANTED to enjoy her for my own benefit. I DID want to be with her and enjoy her, but I always felt guilty for not doing church work. Once God explained what really pleased him, I could take a day off with relish knowing I was in his perfect will, working "priority number three."

I began to take one whole day off for the family each week and later added three extra nights. I guard these times and put them ahead of all other demands. This was very healing to my wife.

#2 Avoid Condemning Words

The second great lesson God taught me was how to avoid "motivation through condemnation."

The Bible says, "Do not let any unwholesome talk come out of your mouths, but only what is helpful for building others up according to their needs, that it may

118

LESSON: CONDEMNING WORDS ERODE RELATIONSHIPS. **STOP** BEFORE THE EROSION CAUSES YOUR HOUSE (FAMILY) TO FALL IN!

benefit those who listen," (Ephesians 4:29 NIV).

For years I tried to motivate my wife with articulate words of put down, pointing out forcefully why she was wrong in word, attitude, or action. I thought I was doing God a favor by "correcting" her, but how wrong I was!

God showed me that many people feel inadequate and that this "fear of being inadequate" erodes an ever deepening chasm in their lives.

One day I was on the verge of really letting my wife "have it" verbally when God stopped me. He said, "Fear of inadequacy is eroding your wife. If you go in today and berate her, you will only reinforce those feelings that she is not good enough. The chasm will be eroded even more quickly—so fast in fact that TODAY your whole house will fall in! You must go in and fill that ditch with encouraging words!"

With that understanding, I was enabled to speak tender words of comfort. I shudder to think of what would have happened had I spoken what I first intended!

One of the most spiritual things we can ever learn is to SHUT UP when we feel like berating our mate! If you win by filleting them with your sharp tongue, don't smirk in your pride. You have foolishly destroyed yourself!

We can learn a great lesson from Abraham. Sarah had begged Abraham for a baby, saying something like this, "Abe, I want a baby so badly. I'm tired of waiting. Take my servant, Hagar, and sleep with her. Perhaps I can raise a family through her."

Abraham probably said, "Honey, I think we should keep waiting. You know what God spoke to me."

Sarah probably said, "I just can't wait anymore or I'll go crazy."

And Abraham responded, "Okay, baby. But remember, this is your idea!"

Thirteen years later Sarah was holding her own baby, Isaac, while Ishmael, Hagar's son through Abraham, stood mocking. Angrily Sarah raised her voice to Abraham and said, "Get rid of that slave woman and her son, for that slave woman's son will never share in the inheritance with my son, Isaac," (Genesis 21:10 NIV).

This was no small marital dispute. The whole marriage was on the line. For thirteen years Ishmael had been the delight of Abraham's heart. This was his son! Get rid of him? Send him away into a trackless wilderness? How easily he could have yelled insults at Sarah in the heat of anger.

Good thing Abraham knew how to SHUT UP. The Bible simply says, "The matter distressed Abraham greatly because it concerned his son," (Genesis 21:10 NIV). Abraham had kept his mouth shut and went on a prayer walk, knowing he needed to hear from God if his marriage was to survive. And God spoke, saying he'd see to it that Ishmael would survive in the desert and become a great nation. But God did say to send him away! Abraham could not have done that without a special word.

But what does a man do when he's "greatly distressed" if he has neglected his relationship with God to the point he can't hear God when he really needs to? HE DOES THE WRONG THING! That is why we must put knowing God as our first priority.

Many times I've been "greatly distressed" and had to take a prayer walk asking God for a special word. Because I loved God and put him first in my life, I would hear. And God NEVER sided with me against my wife! He ALWAYS showed me how to love her in a Christ-like way. My own way would have destroyed us ten times over! How desperately we need to walk with God so that he can give us those special words of grace that defuse explosive situations.

#3 Practice Daily This Five-Point Plan To Supply What Your Mate Needs.

The third great lesson God taught me was the five things my wife needs daily—things he commanded me to supply. These are: encouragement, comfort, tenderness, fellowship and compassion. (See Philippians 2:1-2 NIV.)

When I whined to God that I wasn't getting enough affection from my wife, he said, "Apply the law of first love."

"What's that?" I asked.

"You love me because I first loved you. So if you want to get affection, go be affectionate to your wife."

That day I walked home and made myself display affection when I didn't feel like it. My feelings had been numbed by our sharp verbal ex-changes. But as I daily dispensed hugs and kisses (comfort), God broke the hardened crust from my own heart and deep affection returned. And when affection is displayed daily OUTSIDE the bedroom with no sexual motive, true sexual expressions of oneness will occur in the bedroom at night.

Once I complained to God, "My wife doesn't see anything good in me, only bad. She hates me."

God said, "Go home and make a chart. At the top put, "I SEE SOMETHING GOOD IN YOU". Make a column for you and one for her. Make a line for each day of the month. Then YOU begin to write down what good things you see in her."

I discovered I had become very negative myself because I could hardly think of one good thing to write down about my wife. I was glad I only had to think of one each day. After the first couple of days, I began to think of multiple good things to write but just kept putting down one as instructed. My wife did not write ANYTHING on my side.

"See, God? She DOESN'T see anything good in me!"

"Just keep doing what I told you!" God answered.

About the tenth day I came to the chart and discovered my wife had caught up with me, writing down ten good things about me like.... "he changes his underwear" and "he brushes his teeth." There was no comment like, "He's a great man of God." But I rejoiced, "She DOES see something good in me!"

We finished out the month side by side and soon the bigger compliments (encouragement) began to appear. "He's a good provider." "He's a good father." Again, the change came when I changed.

God wants us to thank and compliment each other every day. That is encouragement! If you sow it, you will reap it.

God taught me that compassion is when you "use your power to help someone." He told me to do at least one kind deed for my wife each day—laundry, vacuuming, dishes, etc. At first, I waited for my wife to rave, "Oh, you marvelous man! Thank you!" That didn't happen. Instead, I learned that if you plant kind deeds you reap kind deeds. If you want compliments plant compliments. I began to reap kind deeds as my wife started doing favors for me.

Soon I was doing the kind deeds not for compliments or reciprocation of kind deeds, but rather for the pure joy

ONCE A DAY

1. DAILY DISPLAY AFFECTION (COMFORT)
2. DAILY GIVE A THANKYOU OR COMPLIMENT (ENCOURAGEMENT)
3. DAILY HAVE A FAMILY ACTIVITY (FELLOWSHIP)
4. DAILY HAVE AN UNHURRIED CONVERSATION (TENDERNESS)
5. DAILY DO KIND DEEDS FOR EACH OTHER (COMPASSION)·

EVERY DAY
LOVE REAPS A SURE REWARD!

of expressing my love for her. Now I eagerly look for ways to bless her as soon as I get up in the morning, when I'm home at noon, and in the evening hours.

God taught me to practice tenderness by having at least one conversation a day where we talk unhurriedly. How important it is to take time just to talk. And husbands, this means put down the paper, turn off the TV, and give your wife the undivided attention she needs.

God defined fellowship as "time together pursuing the same interest." This can be grocery shopping, a game, a devotion, yard work, anything you both enjoy.

At first, I grumbled that my wife wouldn't do the things I enjoyed, but God had no sympathy for me and just told me to bend and do what she enjoyed! And like everything else, you reap what you sow! Now on a typical day we have at least one family activity where we do something together.

One day I said to my wife, "We sure are getting along a lot better because you've changed."

"I didn't change; you did," she answered.

I was about ready to act ignorant and inform her that I had never been the one who needed to change. Then I realized that she had actually complimented me.

"Thanks," I smiled. "I guess I HAVE changed."

And your mate will change, too, if you change and "give your way out of problems". Give what you want to receive. Plant what you want to harvest! And remember God's words to me, "Just keep doing what I told you."

Your Priorities

Let me repeat. First, get your priorities right! Put God first. That means daily devotions, church attendance, and tithing.

Second, take care of your health. Remember, "Do not destroy the work of God for the sake of food," (Romans

14:20 NIV). If you overeat and ruin your girlish figure, ladies, you lay a stumbling block for your mate. Men, if you don't take care of your health, you'll destroy the work of God by dying of some degenerative disease before your time.

Third—your mate. Fourth, your children; fifth, your work; sixth, the brethren.

If your aging parents can take care of themselves, they go on this priority level with the brethren and must NOT come before mate or children! Aged parents who can't take care of themselves go on the same level as children.

Seventh—the lost, the focus of all priorities.

Many marriages are destroyed because "self" becomes the primary priority, taking the place of God.

"Things" also become the "focus" of priorities, becoming what the family pursues. The family is squeezed to death in this vice of selfishness and materialism. But when God orders your priorities—relationships, not things, form every level.

"Better a little with the fear of the Lord than great wealth with turmoil. Better a meal of vegetables where there is love than a fattened calf with hatred," (Proverbs 15:16-17 NIV).

Secondly, stop speaking words that tear down. Memorize this verse: "Do not let any unwholesome talk come out of your mouths, but only what is helpful for building others up according to their needs, that it may benefit those who listen," (Eph. 4:29 NIV).

Five a Day, Every Day

Thirdly, supply five things a day to your mate. Every day display affection outside of the bedroom without building up to love making. Men are horribly negligent in supplying affection to their wives. This makes women resistant to sexual advances. But, if you'll show lots of affection each day—

as often as possible, you'll create an environment for sexual intimacy.

Every day look for a way to tell each other, "You are good."

God taught me, "A guilty person can't meet your need for approval. They can't see you are good because they are too busy thinking how bad they are." So don't tell your mate how bad he or she is. Instead, find things to compliment them about—at least one compliment a day. Miracle habits lead to miracles. God wants us to do these things at least once a day to develop good habits.

Every day have a family activity, something you are mutually interested in. "Each of you should look not only to your own interests, but also to the interests of others," (Phil. 2:4 NIV). It doesn't have to be long—it could be as short as a prayer, or a meal, or a game, or a shopping trip— but do something together every day.

Every day talk to each other. Most women are desperate to have their men act interested enough in them to listen and talk—not to find out quick facts or get advice, but just to talk for talk's sake. And, sir, look at your wife when she talks—give her your full attention. She needs tenderness.

Finally, every day use your power to help, (compassion). Plant one kind and considerate deed after another. Pick up after yourself. Don't leave messes all over. Practice every form of consideration knowing that if you can show unselfish love to those you live with—all other hindrances to prayer will be swept away and nothing will hinder your prayers, (1 Peter 3:7, NIV). And just keep it up. Don't listen when the devil says, "It's not working." God taught me, "LOVE REAPS A SURE REWARD".

Beloved, if you'll DO THESE THINGS you'll find they work. But, none of us do them perfectly. Ultimately, God has to heal marriages.

The Bible tells of four men who carried a paralytic up

on a roof, then lowered him down through the roof before Jesus. Then "seeing their faith" he healed the man (Mark 2:5 KJV). These men didn't give their friend the smoothest trip up on the roof. No doubt they jostled him around quite a bit and most likely caused him some pain. When they lowered him down, one probably let out the rope on his corner faster than the other and perhaps the cot tilted at dangerous angles. But they did get him down in front of Jesus.

Supplying these five things daily is the true way to get your marriage down in front of Jesus. Although you will never do these things perfectly, if you keep trying, you'll be going in the right direction. And Jesus will heal your marriage!

Beloved, remember, an intercessor must be the sweetest person in the church. They must also practice having a sweet spirit at home. This is the foundation for your life of prayer.

13
TRY HARD TO BE RECONCILED

A life of effective prayer is built upon reconciliation.

In its simplest form, to reconcile with someone means to say, "I'm sorry. I was wrong. What can I do to make it right?" Failure to make things right results in frustrated lives until reconciliation occurs.

Every house has a shut off valve to the water supply. If that one valve is closed all the water in the house is shut off. You can turn on the bathroom faucet—but nothing will come out. You can turn on the kitchen faucet, but you'll get nothing but air.

God controls the shut off valve as far as blessings are concerned. If he shuts off the master valve, we can open the faucet of prayer—but nothing happens. We can open the faucet of giving, but no blessings flow because we have given. We can open the faucet of fasting, and still get no results! God shuts off the master valve to blessings when reconciliation has been neglected.

If the Master Valve is shut off through failure to reconcile...fasting, prayer and giving are in vain!

The entire chapter of 2 Samuel 21 deals with reconciliation and contains wonderful lessons for us. Verse one (NIV) reads: "During the reign of David, there was a famine for three successive years; so David sought the face of the Lord." You can be sure David and his people were praying for rain after the first dry year and even more so after the second dry year. Their giving, their fasting, their praying, their sacrifices were increased—but to no avail.

Then David inquired as to why God shut off the master valve. "The Lord said, 'It is on account of Saul and his blood-stained house; it is because he put the Gibeonites to death,'" (2 Samuel 21:1, NIV).

King Saul was David's predecessor. In his misguided zeal for God, Saul had decimated a people (survivors of the Amorites) who had made a peace treaty with Israel. (See Joshua 9.) David had not sinned, yet the famine came during his reign. God was acting as a witness on behalf of the Gibeonites.

David seemed to know that in order for God to bless him he would first have to get the Gibeonites to bless him. If he could make things right with them, and they blessed him, he knew God would turn on the master valve of blessings—and the faucets of prayer, giving, and fasting would work again.

Many Christians think they don't need to be blessed by the people they have wronged. They assume they can walk on, leave conflict unresolved, never say they are sorry, never make it right—and still have God's blessing. They waste their lives trying to get God's blessing when all the time they need to be seeking the blessing of those they have wronged!

When God Witholds

Before we cover David's solution, let's understand the principles involved. We all like to quote: "No good thing does he withhold from those whose walk is blameless," (Psalm 84:11, NIV). However, God does withhold good things when we fail to reconcile because that's not a blameless way to live.

I believe the most neglected command of Christ is Matthew 5:23 (NIV): "Therefore, if you are offering your gift at the altar and there remember that your brother has something against you, leave your gift there in front of the altar. First go and be reconciled to your brother; then come and offer your gift." Few people obey this verse Instead, they tithe and give offerings without reconciling and then grumble, "Tithing doesn't work." To say that is a self indictment. If our giving doesn't "work", it's time to obey Matthew 5:23.

1 Peter 3:7 (NIV) says, "Husbands, in the same way be considerate as you live with your wives, and treat them with respect as the weaker partner and as heirs with you of the gracious gift of life, so that nothing will hinder your prayers." If the husband is disrespectful and inconsiderate to his wife, God will act as a witness against him and will start closing off the master valve of blessing until he reconciles with his wife. Prayer alone won't bring God's blessing.

Fasting, like prayer and giving, can be compared to a faucet in the kitchen or bathroom. It will produce nothing unless God opens the master valve. "Your fasting ends in quarreling and strife, and in striking each other with wicked fists. You cannot fast as you do today and expect your voice to be heard on high," (Isaiah 58:4, NIV). Strife nullifies prayer!

God acts as a witness between you and the party you have wronged. We see this principle in God's Word. "Another thing you do: You flood the Lord's altar with tears. You weep and wail because he no longer pays attention to your offerings or accepts them with pleasure from your hands. You ask, 'Why?' It is because the Lord is acting as the witness between you and the wife of your youth, because you have broken faith with her, though she is your partner, the wife of your marriage covenant.....So guard yourself in your spirit, and do not break faith," (Malachi 2:13-16,NIV).

What does it mean, "Do not break faith"? Electricity must have a complete circuit to flow. If you flip a light switch off, the circuit is broken and the lights go out. Breaking faith means to break a circuit—to disconnect from someone you should be loving.

One day when I was praying with a group of ministers, Pastor Maurice Estrada had a vision. In the vision, as we loved each other, God's arms came around us and his hands locked, creating a circuit. Then as we continued to love each other, the fiery power of God went all the way around through God's arms—swoosh! As we continued to love each other, this current went faster and faster—swoosh, swoosh, swoosh!

Pastor Estrada was excited as he told me what he had seen, but he didn't understand the meaning. I said, "That sounds like a generator to me. In a generator the power goes round and around until it comes out bigger on the other end." God was showing us that as we love each other it becomes the generator for God's power!

Jesus said, "By this will all men know that you are my disciples, if you love one another," (John 13:35, NIV). When we reconcile and bless each other, it brings such powerful blessings from God that everyone recognizes God's hand is upon us!

Psalm 133:1-3 (NIV) emphasizes this truth: "How good and pleasant is it when brothers live together in unity! It is like precious oil poured on the head, running down on the beard, running down on Aaron's beard, down upon the collar of his robes. It is as if the dew of Hermon were falling on Mount Zion. For there the Lord bestows his blessing, even life forevermore." **God bestows his blessing where brethren are blessing each other.**

We must understand this: The blessing from those who have been wronged is equivalent to the blessing of God.

What Must I Do To
Receive Your Blessing?

Let's pick up the story in 2 Samuel 21 again and see
how David reconciled with the Gibeonites. "The King sum-
moned the Gibeonites. 'What shall I do for you? How shall
I make amends so that you will bless the Lord's inheritance?'"(vs. 2,3, NIV). David was most concerned about getting the blessing of the Gibeonites. He knew if he could
reconcile with them so that they would bless Israel, then
God would bless Israel.

The blessing of the people you have wronged will be a
forerunner to the blessings of God just as John the Baptist
prepared the way for the coming of Christ.

We need to make a great effort to reconcile. Consider
how much you need the blessing of people you have
wronged in order to get God's blessing again. Then go after
it! Try hard to be reconciled!

How did the Gibeonites respond to David's question?
"The Gibeonites answered him, 'We have no right to
demand silver or gold from Saul or his family, nor do we
have the right to put anyone in Israel to death.'" "'What do
you want me to do for you?' David asked," (2 Samuel
21:4,5, NIV). Notice, David asked them twice. The first
time it was as if they replied, "It's okay. Just forget it." David
basically was saying, "No! I need your blessing. Now I
insist—what must I do to get your blessing?"

"They answered the king, 'As for the man who
destroyed us and plotted against us so that we have been
decimated and have no place anywhere in Israel, let seven
of his male descendants be given to us to be killed and
exposed before the Lord at Gibeah of Saul—the Lord's chosen one.' So the king said, 'I will give them to you,'" (verse
5, NIV).

This is a powerful example of why we should repent
for the sins of the fathers. Suppose one of these seven had

been ashamed of what his ancestor, King Saul, had done. What if he had gone to the Gibeonites and said, "I'm so sorry for what Saul did to you. I want to help you. I'll serve you and use my recourses to bless you." Do you think the Gibeonites would have asked that such a man be put to death? No way! But none of these men had sought to reconcile the wrongs done by their ancestor.

It is a dangerous false assumption to assume that the sins of our ancestors have no effect on us in this life. What if we are praying for revival in America and God doesn't answer prayer for the land because of sins done to the blacks or American Indians by our founding fathers? Are we descended from a slave owner? Are we descended from a pioneer who shot Indians for sport? Shouldn't we seek to bless those our ancestors treated badly so that a judgment similar to what fell on Saul's seven male descendants never befalls us?

Digging Up The Past

Leviticus 26:39-42 (NIV) makes the case for true reconciliation: "Those of you who are left will waste away in the lands of their enemies because of their sins; also because of their fathers' sins they will waste away.

"But if they will confess their sins and the sins of their fathers—their treachery against me and their hostility toward me, which made me hostile toward them so that I sent them into the land of their enemies—then when their uncircumcised hearts are humbled and they pay for their sin, I will remember my covenant with Jacob and my covenant with Isaac and my covenant with Abraham, and I will remember the land."

In the New Covenant God has made with us, Christ has paid for our sins. We can't "pay back" anything to God for our sins. But we could do something kind to those we or our ancestors wronged. That would show genuine repentance.

As the Gibeonites requested, the seven male descendants of Saul were killed and left exposed for many months. But the mother of two of these men camped out by their bodies and kept the birds and the scavengers away. She did this from the beginning of harvest until the rain poured down on their bodies. I believe this means from early summer until fall she kept this vigilance of love.

David heard what this loving mother was doing for her dead sons. But before he properly buried their bones David went to Jabesh Gilead and dug up the bones of King Saul and his son Jonathan.

This is very significant but to understand it you must know a bit of Bible history. King Saul had disobeyed God so often that God gave him over to the Philistines who killed him and several of his sons on Mount Gilboa. They took his headless body and nailed it to the wall of Beth Shan. "Sha'an" was the Phoenician serpent god—Satan!

The citizens of Jabesh Gilead, however, remembered how Saul in his youth had rescued them from Nahash the Ammonite who had wanted to enslave them and gouge out their eyes. They marched all night and daringly took down Saul's body from the wall, escaped, and buried him in their town.

Now, years later, David goes back to Jabesh Gilead and digs up Saul's bones. He brings Saul's and Jonathan's bones, along with the bones of Saul's seven male descendants who had been killed and exposed to satisfy the Gibeonites and buries them all in the tomb of Saul's father Kish, at Zela in Benjamin.

2 Samuel 21:14 (NIV) records: **"After that, God answered prayer in behalf of the land."**

Why dig up the past? The Gibeonites were now blessing Israel. Rain had begun to fall upon the exposed bodies. But the full blessing of God upon Israel didn't come until David reburied Saul's bones with honor and somehow released the past once and for all.

Often the unreconciled past has been buried and forgotten, but prayers are still hindered because there is lingering bitterness. To be buried right the past must be dug up, reconciled, and forgiven. Both parties need to be treated respectfully—the victim and the victimizer, the innocent and the guilty. Unforgiven burials are no good! The past needs to be reconciled and then buried with dignity. When David did this, God answered prayer for the land. It was finally over.

When To Reconcile

There are several kinds of reconciliation we must seek.

1. We must seek to reconcile past wrongs done by our predecessors or ancestors. David had to right the wrong done by his predecessor. Sometimes pastors have to reconcile with people wounded by the previous pastor. As an American descendant of white Europeans, I'm interested in blessing blacks and native Americans. If they bless me, it will be equivalent to the blessing of God!

2. We must seek to reconcile what we ourselves have done wrong.

A. Directly. If you wronged a person directly, try to make it right. Say you are sorry, ask forgiveness, and then say, "What must I do for you to bless me?" If possible, do it.

B. Indirectly. This is harder, and not quite as necessary. But if your sin against someone else indirectly affected and hurt other people, you should ask their forgiveness too. Good hunters like to clean their rifles so they shoot really straight. Why not keep your heart as clean as your rifle?

In 1991 God gave me a fiery anointing which burns in my hands and my feet. Sometimes this anointing results is supernatural healings, but more often it sets people free from the spiritual oppression of evil spirits. The more I discovered about deliverance the more zealous I became. Gradually I moved from being a worshipper to being mainly a warrior. I began to focus more on exposing the devil than revealing Christ. These and other mistakes opened a door for the devil to oppress the church I pastored.

Within two years of receiving that wonderful anointing my false assumptions had accumulated to the point that I sinned ignorantly. Many people were negatively affected. It took me months to understand my errors, my ignorant sins, and my false assumptions. But when I did, I admitted it on my radio show, from my pulpit, and sent letters of apology to everyone I could think of who had been directly or indirectly affected. God kept bringing different people to mind for me to contact. For the next three years I wrote to different people, asking forgiveness, admitting my errors, and sending them a list of deliverance corrections I had learned.

God helps us make lemonade from our lemons. Now God uses me to bring balance and correction in the same areas where I used to be imbalanced and in error. Our emphasis should always be: "Major on revealing Christ. Minor on exposing the devil. Major on worship of God, minor on warfare."

Some people forgave me, and some didn't. My point is—I tried very hard to be reconciled. We must be careful not to think, "What's the use? They'll never forgive me anyway." Such a thought would be a judgment against their heart—an evil thought to be rejected. My business was to clear my own conscience, to do my part, to try hard.

Our efforts to reconcile won't be done perfectly because we aren't perfect people. But it's worth it to try hard. We must not be discouraged when others refuse to ask forgiveness for their part in strife or conflict. Nor can we give up if they continue to judge us and refuse our requests to be forgiven. We "try hard to be reconciled" (Luke 12:58) because we love Jesus enough to obey him!

We only pretend to be spiritual if we act like we never do anything wrong. The more spiritual we get, the more we'll find ourselves admitting our errors, mistakes, and sins. I used to think spiritual people rarely goofed up. Now I identify with James who wrote, "*We all* stumble in many ways," (James 3:2, NIV). He was an apostle, the head of the Jerusalem church and he still found himself stumbling—not in just a few ways, but in many! But he had grown enough in Christ to admit it.

3. *Seek to reconcile with those who have wronged you!* For me, this is the most difficult. I'd rather forget it. But seeking to reconcile with someone who has wronged you is an act of compassion. Why? Because they could vainly spend the rest of their lives trying to get God to bless them or answer their prayers when it is really your blessing they need.

Jesus said, "If your brother sins against you, go and show him his fault, just between the two of you. If he listens to you, you have won your brother over. But if he will not listen, take one or two others along, so that 'every matter may be established by the testimony of two or three witnesses.' If he refuses to listen to them, tell it to the church; and if he refuses to listen even to the church, treat him as you would a pagan or a tax collector. I tell you the truth, whatever you bind on earth will be bound in heaven, and whatever you loose on earth will be loosed in heaven. Again, I tell you that if two of you on earth agree about anything you ask for, it will be done for you by my Father in heaven. For where two or three come together in my name, there am I with them," (Matthew 18:15-20, NIV).

Notice how Jesus ties answered prayer to completed reconciliation. They are not disconnected subjects. Reconciliation leads directly to answered prayer. Let's look at the steps Jesus outlined.

How To Reconcile With Those Who Wronged You

A. Go to the person who wronged you, not to others to complain how you were mistreated, (see verse 15). When you go, go to pursue reconciliation. Don't set out to shame him, hurt him, gore him, express anger or contempt, etc. If you hurt him back, you compound the problem. Then you'll both have to say you are sorry and make things right in order to get the circuit repaired! A fence with two broken strands of wire takes twice as long to fix as a fence with only one broken.

A certain lady was shocked at Abraham Lincoln's desire to make peace with Southern Rebel leaders. "You should be destroying them!" she snorted. Lincoln said, "Do I not destroy my enemies when I make them my friends?" Memorize that line! It's profound.

B. Keep pursuing reconciliation, (see verse 16). Take two people with you—and go in a sweet spirit. You're going to reconcile, remember, not to have a hanging.

C. "Tell it to the church," (verse 17) You really are serious about this, aren't you! Good! Why all the bother? His failure to reconcile with you will permanently mess up his life, and we can't have that, can we? (I suggest you tell it to a church board rather than in a congregational service.)

D. Avoid PLOM disease. (Poor Little Ol' Me) If they wrong you, feel sorry for them, not yourself. After all, being wronged won't hinder your prayers or your offerings one bit! If they won't reconcile after those steps, treat them like a tax collector. That means, be nice, pray for them, but don't trust them. Treat them as you would a lost person.

The Apostle Paul wrote, "Warn a divisive person once, and then warn him a second time. After that, have nothing to do with him. You may be sure that such a man is warped and sinful; he is self-condemned," (Titus 3:10, NIV). It's very difficult to reconcile with a divisive person who is under the influence of demonic spirits that are attempting to tear up the church. In such cases the steps given in Matthew 18:15-20 are inappropriate. However, even in such heart-breaking cases, we should pray fervently that God will deliver these people from the grip of totally unreasonable divisive spirits.

Remember, don't make reconciliation doubly hard by wronging those who wronged you. Keep it simple. "Do not repay evil with evil or insult with insult, but with blessing, because to this you were called so that you may inherit a blessing," (1 Peter 3:9, NIV).

"If someone strikes you on one cheek, turn to him the other also. If someone takes your cloak, do not stop him from taking your tunic," (Luke 6:29, NIV).

The apostle Paul wrote, "If it is possible, as far as it depends on you, live at peace with everyone. Do not take revenge, my friends, but leave room for God's wrath, for it is written: 'It is mine to avenge; I will repay,' says the Lord. On the contrary: 'If your enemy is hungry, feed him; if he is thirsty, give him something to drink. In doing this, you will heap burning coals on his head.' Do not be overcome by evil, but overcome evil with good," (Romans 12:18-20, NIV).

No matter what mean things people do to you, how many team up against you, how vicious they are, or how carefully they plot against you—no one can ruin your life but you.

Once I was fuming about a certain lady whose actions were causing me a great deal of trouble and pain. I complained to God, "If you don't do something about her she's going to ruin my life and ministry!"

God instantly spoke to me and said, "The only thing that could ever ruin your life and ministry would be your own hard heart."

I quickly began to change my attitude, soften my heart, pray for that lady, and made an effort to be kind and gracious.

Have you bought into the lie of Satan that someone else has ruined or is ruining your life? Remember, it's not what others do to us that can ruin us, but only our wrong responses. If we respond in love, every stumbling stone that others throw our way will become a stepping stone.

Our Ministry and Our Message

Finally, remember that for a Christian the word "reconciliation" is a defining word, as the Bible makes clear: "God has reconciled us to himself through Christ and gave us the ministry of reconciliation.....He has committed to us the message of reconciliation," (2 Corinthians 5:19, NIV). "But now he has reconciled you by Christ's physical body through death to present you holy in his sight, without blemish and free from accusation—if you continue in your-faith, established and firm, not moved from the hope held out in the gospel," (Colossians 1:22, NIV).

Looking at these verses, we see that reconciliation is our ministry, our message, and our position in Christ. Will you "try hard to be reconciled" (Luke 12:58)? Try hard to reconnect the broken circuits—the damaged relationships. Be careful not to break any more circuits.

Those who neglect these commands turn off switch after switch, breaking circuit after circuit and then wonder why it's so dark in their lives. Your life won't go totally dark by breaking a circuit with one person. It's more like switching a light off in one room. But if you keep up that pattern, every broken relationship is like turning out the lights in another room of your life. Those who habitually refuse to admit they were wrong are people who have turned the lights out in their own lives and now live in darkness.

It takes two to reconcile. We can only take care of our part. Remember, "As far as it depends on you, live at peace with all men," (Romans 12:18, NIV). If you practice these truths, God will open the master valve of blessing so that your prayers, fasting, and giving are all abundantly blessed.

As intercessors, we must be the sweetest spirits in the church—the first to forgive others, and the first to admit when we are wrong.

The apostle John wrote, "Dear friends, if our hearts do not condemn us, we have confidence before God and receive from him anything we ask, because we obey his commands and do what pleases him," (1 John 3:21, NIV).

Our nation and our world are in desperate need of prayer, but who will be the kind of person God always hears? Prayer without a loving heart is like faith without corresponding action—it is dead. Make every effort to practice these truths so that your heart will be pure and your spirit sweet. Then your communication lines with God will work wonderfully. You'll be able to hear from him, and God will be waiting eagerly to hear the kind of loving prayers you pray.

One night when I was having a meeting with my prayer partners, I received what I call, "A Fax From God." It was as if a whole page of God's words were faxed into my spirit instantly, and I had to take the time to read it. The essence of what God said to me was that the desire in my heart to bring God massive glory is really a call to prayer.

After I deciphered what God was saying to me, I preached a sermon about the five ways to bring God glory.

The *first* way I call "Basic Glory." We bring God glory when we love our families, open doors for the elderly, practice consideration while driving, etc.

The *second* way is "Added glory". We bring God this kind of glory when we win a soul to Christ. Then there are two of us to bring God Basic Glory!

The *third* way to bring God glory is called "Multiplied Glory". In the book of Acts 5,000 souls were "added" to the church in one day. But the believers were not "multiplied" until chapter six when additional leaders were raised up.

We multiply glory to God when we train a leader.

The *fourth* way to bring God glory is through effective prayer. I call it "Great Glory" because when we pray, we open a door for the involvement of the Holy Spirit in the affairs of men—and he can do the really great things!

The *fifth* way to bring God glory is to be faithful for a lifetime—always living passionately for God. I call this "Compound Interest Glory" because it adds up like compound interest. It may seem insignificant early on in life, but if we live in love with God for a lifetime—faithfully doing God's will—it will amount to a whole lot over a lifetime!

Add these five ways together and you have MASSIVE GLORY! Why go to all the trouble to have a pure heart— just so you can get more answers to prayer for yourself? That's not the primary reason. The main reason to practice the truths in this book is so that your life will result in massive glory coming to God. May it be so.

APPENDIX:

SWEET SPIRIT VERSES

Here is a collection of what I call "sweet spirit verses". These are loaded with spiritual immunities to the dread diseases of disloyalty, a demonic point of view (critical spirit), bitterness, and the like.

If you would really like to BE an intercessor, I strongly urge you to take your Bible and this list, and mark each scripture. Write beside it, "SWEET SPIRIT". This will help you notice these verses when you read, and help you find many others that are not listed here.

Many Christians try to collect verses on healing or prosperity or blessing of some kind in order to get what they want. But, if you'll FIRST OF ALL collect verses on having the kind of heart Jesus commanded in the Beatitudes, you'll find a life of prayer becomes easy and natural.

When all the Beatitudes are added together, they equal a sweet spirit! With that in mind, read the Sermon on the Mount (Matt. 5-7). Notice that each of Christ's commands can only be kept by those who have the kind of spiritual attitude spoken of at the start of the sermon. Ask yourself, "Which of the Beatitudes can keep this command?"

The entire Sermon on the Mount is based on these spiritual attitudes. If you would like the kind of prayer life that receives when it asks, a life above anger and strife, a life of worry-free living, and the ability to stand strong through any storm then CONCENTRATE on these verses. Treasure them in your heart, think about them often, memorize them, and above all PRACTICE THEM.

Genesis 9:20-27
Exodus 9:20-27
Numbers 14:36-37
1 Samuel 12:23
1 Samuel 22:14
Job 23:30
Psalm 15:1-5
Psalm 17:1 & 3
Psalm 19:12-13
Psalm 19:14
Psalm 24:3-4
Psalm 34:15
Psalm 35:12-14 (KJV)
Psalm 37:8
Psalm 37:37
Psalm 72:21-22
Psalm 101:5
Psalm 106:23
Psalm 109:4
Psalm 133:1
Psalm 141:5
Psalm 1:23 (NAS)
Proverbs 6:16-19
Proverbs 10:2
Proverbs 10:18
Proverbs 11:18
Proverbs 12:18
Proverbs 12:20
Proverbs 14:30
Proverbs 15:4
Proverbs 15:13a
Proverbs 15:15b
Proverbs 15:16-17
Proverbs 15:26
Proverbs 17:9
Proverbs 17:22
Proverbs 17:1
Proverbs 17:9
Proverbs 21:21
Proverbs 29:5
Ecclesiastes 5:1-2
Jeremiah 9:1
Jeremiah 9:7
Jeremiah 13:17

Jeremiah 14:17
Lamentations 2:11
Obadiah 12:15b
Matthew 5:7-9
Matthew 5:44-47
Mark 11:25
John 1:16
John 5:41 & 44
John 13:34-35
John 14:15
John 14:21 & 23
John 15:7
John 17:9-10 (KJV)
John 17:23
John 20:27
Acts 13:22b
Romans 1:9-11
Romans 8:28
Romans 14:1
Romans 14:13
Romans 15:1-2
Romans 15:7
Romans 15:30
Romans 16:17-18
1 Corinthians 1:10
1 Corinthians 4:12-13
1 Corinthians 5:11
1 Corinthians 6:9-10
1 Corinthians 8:1
1 Corinthians 11:32
1 Corinthians 13:1-7
2 Corinthians 2:4
2 Corinthians 13:7 & 9b
2 Corinthians 13:11
Galatians 5:13b
Galatians 5:15
Galatians 5:19-21
Galatians 5:22-23
Galatians 5:26
Galatians 6:1
Ephesians 1:16-17
Ephesians 1:19
Ephesians 3:16-19
Ephesians 4:2-3

Ephesians 4:15-16
Ephesians 4:26-27
Ephesians 4:29
Ephesians 4:31
Ephesians 4:32
Ephesians 5:1-2
Ephesians 5:22-33
Ephesians 6:18
Philippians 1:9-11
Philippians 2:1-2
Philippians 2:3-4
Philippians 2:14-15
Philippians 2:20-21
Philippians 4:2-8
Colossians 1:9-12
Colossians 3:12-15
Colossians 3:18-21
Colossians 4:2-4
Colossians 4:12-13
1 Thessalonians 3:12
1 Thessalonians 3:13
2 Thessalonians 1:11
1 Timothy 2:1-2
2 Timothy 2:19b
2 Timothy 2:24-26
2 Timothy 4:5
Titus 2:3
Titus 3:10-11
Philemon 6
Philemon 22
Hebrews 3:12-13
Hebrews 5:9
Hebrews 12:5-6
Hebrews 12:15
Hebrews 13:20-21
James 1:26
James 3:2
James 3:6
James 3:16-18
James 5:16
1 Peter 3:7-9
2 Peter 1:5-11
1 John 3:14-17
1 John 5:15-16